PERCY
BUSH

PERCY BUSH

Welsh Rugby's Little Marvel

KEN POOLE

First impression: 2015

© Copyright Ken Poole, 2015

The contents of this book are subject to copyright, and may
not be reproduced by any means, mechanical or electronic,
without the prior, written consent of the publishers.

Cover design: Y Lolfa

ISBN: 978 1 78461 121 7

Published and printed in Wales
on paper from well-maintained forests by
Y Lolfa Cyf., Talybont, Ceredigion SY24 5HE
website www.ylolfa.com
e-mail ylolfa@ylolfa.com
tel 01970 832 304
fax 832 782

Contents

Preface

WALES, AS A passionate rugby nation, has had a long-standing love affair with its outside halves. Players such as Barry John, Jonathan Davies, Neil Jenkins, Phil Bennett and James Hook are regarded as greats from recent eras. The 1940s and 1950s saw Cliff Morgan and Carwyn James compete for the Number 10 position – in the 1930s Cliff Jones was a hero, along with Jerry O'Shea in the 1920s. Before the First World War, in the first Golden Era, Bush, Jenkins, Jones, Bancroft, and Trew, among others, filled the outside half boots at various times.

In each era, there was a great debate on who was the better Number 10, and who should be selected: Bush, Jones or Trew, in the pre-First World War era; Carwyn James or Cliff Morgan in the 1940s/50s; David Watkins or Barry John in 1960s; and then Barry John or Phil Bennett in the 1970s; Gareth Davies or Malcolm Dacey in the 1980s; Jonathan Davies or Neil Jenkins in the 1990s; and Stephen Jones, James Hook, Dan Biggar or Rhys Priestland more recently.

One thing all supporters could agree upon was the criteria and qualities the Wales outside half needed. These would generally include the following:

- Matchwinner
- Slight in stature

- Ability to sidestep
- Exciting runner
- A character on and off the field
- Often a leader or captain
- Place kicking and drop goal expertise
- Confidence and style
- Internationally recognised

Most of the outside halves referred to above could meet most, if not all, of the criteria. Max Boyce, the bard of Wales, referred to the 'outside half factory' to highlight the number and quality of Number 10s Wales has produced since the early part of the twentieth century. However, any factory producing top-quality models, and particularly outside halves, needs a mould to work on; a mould to model others, and one which could be used by spectators, media and coaches alike to benchmark other Number 10s against.

Who created the first mould, and set the quality standards from which we benchmark Welsh Number 10s today? Certainly Percy Bush, who represented Wales eight times in the first Golden Era, captained Cardiff RFC, was the first British Lion to score 100 points on a tour, and was one of the first truly international rugby players and one of the greatest rugby characters, can make a strong claim to be the mould from which all subsequent Welsh Number 10s were modelled. His claim may appear weak, particularly for someone who only represented his country on eight occasions. However, Bush was an extraordinary character, and while the politics of the then Welsh Football Union appeared to conspire to restrict his appearances for

Wales, he was recognised in the international rugby world as an extraordinary talent and rugby personality, 'the inimitable, versatile, ubiquitous Percy Bush'.

Townsend Collins, 'Dromio' of the *South Wales Argus*, who saw Bush, his contemporaries, and other contenders up to the time of the Second World War play, summarised Bush's play as follows:

> He was a genius – at his best amazing in audacity… and skill – but he was variable, temperamental, and erratic. He made too many mistakes, had too many bad days, to be given first place, yet on his great days for club and country, and there were many, he was superlative.

Collins then goes on to highlight his attributes:

> He was a wonderful kicker, with supreme confidence in himself and his dropped goals won many a game, his touch finding was accurate and he was a wonderful runner who… seemed to be able to evade tacklers at will. He could sidestep, dodge or swerve away from opponents – he often left them standing by the suddenness and unexpectedness of his change of direction. He also had the very power of being able to stop dead, so that would-be tacklers rushing down on him rushed past him beat themselves by their own momentum.

He went on to describe Bush as one of the best halfbacks of the past 50 years. His analysis of Bush could have covered some of the play of Cliff Morgan, David Watkins, Barry John, Phil Bennett, Jonathan Davies and Stephen Jones in their prime.

It was the insightful New Zealand press, during the 1904 Anglo-Welsh tour, which managed to decode and enunciate Bush's attributes in the early part of the century so clearly. The *Otago Witness*, following the Otago/Southland game, described him thus:

> Bush is just Bush and if you can imagine a man of medium size as brilliant and clever as Morry Wood [a local outside half] with a lot of originalities besides, you have Bush the champion. He can dodge either way at full speed, is very quick off the mark, makes a hard pass sent him a good one... passes quickly to the right and left... He sometimes turns like a hare at top speed and after running a yard or two gets his opponents moving in the wrong direction, suddenly darts back and starts his three-quarters on one of their deadly passing rushes and is there to receive the last pass if wanted. Besides all that he kicks well... either foot and has the habit of dropping goals at all angles.

A rugby correspondent in one of the London newspapers, writing in December 1906 prior to the Wales v South Africa game at St Helen's, Swansea, also grappled with Percy's strengths and weaknesses. Looking forward to the game, he cites three reasons why Wales would win: Gwyn Nicholls, Percy Bush and J C Dyke, the Penarth full back. Referring to Percy he quotes, 'Bush can win a match on his own. There is not a half playing with quite his faculty for making an opening.' Then he goes on to identify his weaknesses. 'His great faults are a way of taking things too easily and a tendency to drop at goal when of the two scoring choices a pass to his threes is correct football.'

He then goes on in the article to defend Percy's drop goals, suggesting selfishness is not the motive, but the high chance of success with the goal, compared to the potential errors those receiving the pass could make. The author then goes on to highlight his other attributes, claiming that Percy 'is however far from being only a goal dropper'. He then goes on to describe one of Percy's electric runs employed when he is running at a full back. 'It is not a swerve or a right-to-left foot or vice versa dodge, or a feint to pass or a change of foot. It is just a peculiar way of leaning away from the full back just as the latter has made his drive to tackle.'

The author quotes one full back who played against Percy who suggested, 'You just grasp the air, he in some extraordinary way leans backwards or steps backwards, although apparently coming fast and straight, and in a moment is off round you.' The full back concluded by stating, 'this trick left him, lion like, grasping the shadow in a most mysterious manner'.

Writing in 1993, rugby writer Frank Keating, in his review of great fly halves, summarised Bush as follows: 'He [Bush] seems to have been the finished article with shiny brass knobs on; tactical control, cocksure close-quarter running; pluperfect presentation of the pass; unflinching in the tackle and geometric and teasing when kicking in the attack.'

It is my contention that Bush set the standard against which all subsequent Number 10s have been benchmarked.

This book is an attempt to not just highlight the career of Bush, and set out his rugby contribution to Wales, Cardiff, Australia, New Zealand and France, but also to place it in the context of his family and the social and economic environment that produced him, and 'of the concepts of sporting excellence he represented'. Bush and his remarkable family were a product of Edwardian Wales and particularly Cardiff, the 'Coal Metropolis'. Like many great sportsmen and women, Bush's personality, his supreme confidence, charm, approach to 'scientific thinking and rugby', leadership skills, captaincy, arrogance and adventurism, were nurtured and developed within the context of his family. They were, like many other Edwardian families, able to challenge traditional convention and exploit their abilities in this age of science and adventure. In fact, the charm and confidence of Bush may have infuriated traditionalists and officials in the early Welsh Football Union (but not the spectators), and may have been one of the reasons put forward by rugby writers then and today as to why his career was restricted to eight international caps for Wales.

Percy Bush and his family not only made a major impact on sport in Cardiff and Wales, but also exported their skills beyond Wales to include: big game hunting in the former colony of Kenya; nurturing Edwardian artists; exhibiting at the Royal Academy; firmly establishing the roots of technical education in Cardiff and Newport; promoting Welsh industry overseas; and standing up for Pacifist principles during two world wars. A remarkable family, with a remarkable story.

The last link with Bush – his daughter Coralie – died in 1993. The family home in Romilly Crescent, Canton, is now a residential home.

Bush was one of the first popular Cardiff rugby heroes created by the local press and endorsed by supporters inside and outside of Wales. The affection shown towards him in letters from supporters and dignitaries across the United Kingdom and referred to later in this book is quite remarkable. A sheet of the 'Captain's March' music, which was composed in his honour by the Tongwynlais Silver Band, is on display at Cardiff RFC's museum, while there are still a number of older Cardiff supporters who can recall a popular ditty sung by their fathers and grandfathers, which commemorated Percy's performance against Ireland in 1907. The tune is lost but the words were as follows:

> Molly dear, a pint of beer, a Woodbine and a match, Dai and me have been to see a grand old football match, Percy Bush, he scored a goal and shoved the Irish on their 'ole. Are we downhearted? No!

In writing and researching this book, I have been staggered by the number of people, both young and old, inside and outside of Wales, who are familiar with aspects of Percy Bush's career – despite him only playing eight games for Wales and the last just over 100 years ago.

His reputation among Cardiff rugby supporters is still strong, as his elevation to Cardiff Rugby Club's Hall of Fame can testify. His name still appears, one of the few outside the modern era, in the British Lions list of points scorers. There are not many players (in any sport) whose skill and unique contribution to the game, are still being recognised over 100 years later. As recently as 2004, following the famous victory by London Wasps against Toulouse in the Heineken Cup final, Huw Richards, writing for the *Financial Times*, opened his match report by reminding his readers that: 'Frenchmen have long revered Percy Bush,' and he goes on to describe Percy's fumble against the 1905 All Blacks, comparing it to the blunder by Clément Poitrenaud of Toulouse when he failed to ground the ball in time, allowing Rob Howley (a former Cardiff player) to win the touchdown and the game. Percy was one of the first truly internationally recognised players who was not only regarded as one of the greats in his own country, but throughout the United Kingdom, Australia, New Zealand, and latterly France. This is why his name and style of play are still acknowledged by supporters a century after his last game for Wales.

CHAPTER 1

It's in the Genes

PERCY WAS BORN in Cardiff on 23 June 1879, a product of the late Victorian era. This period of the city's history, up to 1914, saw Cardiff establish a reputation as the coal metropolis of the world. The population in 1851 was 20,000, but by 1911 it was 182,000. Like the Klondike, Cardiff attracted people from all over the world, all looking to access the wealth and opportunities created by the coal and shipping owners, particularly the Bute family, who were generating enormous amounts of wealth in this former fishing village. As Martin Daunton highlights:

> ... between 1801 and 1911 there was a huge change in the economy and society of Cardiff, from a small market town with purely local trade to a major port with worldwide ramifications; from a village huddled around the castle to a large city with a radius of 2 to 3 miles. The changes this involved were immense.

The period from 1900 to 1914 was a remarkable time in the life of Wales, in which significant progress was made in sports, arts and education. Historian John Davies highlighted the period as a golden age in boxing and rugby. There was also:

... a marked growth in the social conscience and a number of humanitarian bodies were founded to challenge the evils of the age... there was growing vitality in the cultural scene. In the arts, Welsh horizons were expanding... In the field of architecture, they were splendid advances in Wales including... the Neo-baroque magnificence of the City Hall, Cardiff... the achievements of Welsh scholarship were particularly remarkable. The National Museum of Wales and the National Library came into being... in 1907.

For the first time the people with enquiring minds in Wales were asking questions and getting the answers. This thirst for knowledge was not just confined to the middle and upper classes. In the working-class district of Splott in Cardiff, for example, steelworkers established the Roath Carlylian Club and Institute Society in 1892 to 'enquire into and follow the principles advocated by the philosopher Thomas Carlyle'.

The confidence of the city is exemplified by a report in the *Cardiff Times* in 1908 which boasts: 'It is both ancient and modern; Celtic and Cosmopolitan; progressive; wealthy; enterprising and a centre of learning. There is a Metropolitan ring about its large ideas and "go" which makes all other Welsh towns seem parochial in comparison.'

The city fathers, imbued with this confidence, were also keen to raise the status of the city and improvements were made to the physical infrastructure, such as housing and transport. There was also a desire to focus on the role of education to improve the quality of knowledge and to tackle the insatiable demand from citizens and businesses for technical education. The city and its region, with economic growth ambitions, needed technical skills to encourage this growth. Cardiff and its city fathers needed someone to drive forward technical education and they turned to James Bush, a Carmarthen man steeped in art and design qualifications. These would impress a university appointments' panel today, and included: geometry, machine construction, building construction, mathematics, mechanics, steam, acoustics, light and heat, magnetism, electricity, chemistry and navigation. No better person, then, to drive forward Cardiff's technical education plan.

James Bush was born in Carmarthen in 1844. He was educated at the Lancastrian School and was later apprenticed as a pupil teacher. He attended the Carmarthen School of Art, where he was successful in winning medals for various branches of drawing in science and art in competitions organised by the South Kensington Art Department. In 1863 he entered Bangor Training College, and the following year he continued his training at Cheltenham Normal College.

He arrived in Cardiff in 1865 to take up a post at the invitation of Peter Price, the founder and honorary secretary of the Cardiff Free Library. These were speculative classes established in two rooms at the St Mary Street Free Library building. Mr Bush's salary was dependant on the number of pupils' fees he could attract, and the grants from the South Kensington Science and Art Department, which were triggered by good results in the annual examinations. The *Cardiff and Merthyr Guardian*, in December 1868, extolled the virtues of James Bush's science and arts' classes, suggesting that if it continued and fostered, it 'will effect wonders 'ere long'. The newspaper goes on to argue for more space for the growing classes stating that, 'There is growing taste in Cardiff for science and art but the accommodation is defective', and emphasising strongly, 'there is no town in the Empire in which there is greater scope for Art to shape its end than in Cardiff'. The classes and Bush's teaching proved very successful, with pupils winning many national and local competitions in drawing, art, gas manufacture, carpentry and joinery and mechanical engineering, and the classes were moved to larger accommodation in the Royal Arcade, then to the new library building, and afterwards to Dumfries Place, and finally to the Technical College in Cathays Park. Later, Cardiff Technical College was established in 1916 in Cathays Park, becoming the University of Wales Institute of Science and Technology, which is now incorporated into Cardiff University. Among James' students was T John, father of Sir William Goscombe John RA, who was then a wood carver at Cardiff Castle.

James Bush was also a playing member of Cardiff Rugby Football Club in 1877–8 and a playing member of Cardiff Cricket Club, captain of the combined south Wales chess team, and a founder of Cardiff Naturalists' Society. He was a sportsman, academic and educationalist and was at the heart of these emerging initiatives, all designed to bring knowledge and progress to the growing population of Cardiff.

While training in Cheltenham in 1864 he met his wife Fanny, who was a qualified arts mistress, and she supported James in organising and delivering technical education in the city. She also taught art at Howells School, Llandaff, between 1892 and 1920. Like James, she also supported and contributed to other initiatives within the city. She acted for many years as honorary secretary for the Glamorgan branch of the Welsh Industries Association. The branch was supported by the wives of the great and the good, and included Lady Bute and Lady Plymouth, who gave freely of their time and money to promote Welsh industry. The Welsh Industries Association, for example, provided practical tuition for weavers to study dyes, which resulted in woven Welsh fabrics having its reputation enhanced across the Empire. Exhibitions were hosted which encouraged competition among Welsh businesses – it was an early example of the promotion of Welsh industry, 70 years later inherited by the former Welsh Development Agency. Writing in the *Hywelian Magazine* following her death, her daughter, Ethel Maud, recalls her role as wife and mother and her public service duties for the School of Art, the Welsh Industries Association, League of Mercy and Cambridge local examinations. Ethel then goes on to have a swipe at the restrictions imposed on women, by highlighting that the public duties and social activities of her mother would have been lost, 'If the married women's sphere were restricted as sentimentalists and certain economists would wish'.

While Percy was born at 37 Rawdon Place, Canton, Cardiff, in 1879, the Bush family finally settled at their family home, 15 Romilly Crescent, Canton, in 1890, a home in which the family lived in until the death of Coralie, Percy's daughter, in 1993. Like other Victorian middle-class families, the Bush family's passion for knowledge and progress was evident. They had four sons, Archibald, Reggie, Freddie and Percy, and a daughter, Ethel Maud.

Reginald, the eldest, became headmaster of the Bristol Municipal School of Art. Frederick became organising inspector and director of art in the West Riding of Yorkshire (he also lectured in the university), while Archibald, Percy's younger brother, became executive engineer responsible for designing the drainage system for Mombasa Island, Kenya, in 1897, and later turned to 'big game hunting' to supplement his income. In correspondence with his family he regularly complained about his superintendent, Mr Reynolds, who restricted access to lucrative safaris. Archibald also highlighted why they were so lucrative, claiming he could 'sell elephant tusks for at least £100'. He established a worldwide reputation in his work and eventually served as borough engineer in Lower Hutt, New Zealand. Archibald died in March 1933 after retiring to South Africa, leaving a widow, Edith Fanny.

As noted, Reginald was appointed headmaster of the Bristol School of Art in 1895 (later called the Bristol Municipal School of Art) and under his leadership the school thrived. Reginald was trained at the Royal College of Art, and enhanced the relationship between the arts school and academy, and an all-male artist group in Bristol known as the Bristol Savages. In 1893 he won the British Institution Scholarship for Engineering. In 1898 he was elected an Associate of the Royal Society of Painters, Etchers and Engravers. On Reginald's retirement, in 1934, the School of Art was widely recognised as a leading arts school. While at the school Reginald tutored several prominent etchers, such as Stanley Anderson, Malcolm Osborne, Nathaniel Parks, and Dorothy Woollard. Reginald's assistant, E Willis

Paige, was also a celebrated etcher. Margaret Lindsay Williams, who went on to become a famous portrait painter, also came under the tutorship of Reginald Bush. Sheena Stoddard, in *Impressions Bristol Etchers 1910–1935* comments: '...that the thorough teaching of Reginald Bush launched some artists on national careers and that other, lesser artists were inspired by the quality of work exhibited by him, his colleagues and former pupils'. Today, paintings by Reginald Bush can be found in art galleries around the world, such as *Mill Stream at Llandaff* which is exhibited at the National Gallery of Canada.

Not to be outdone, Percy's sister, Ethel Maud, born in 1874, matriculated into the University of London (many students in this period began their studies there) in June 1892 passing in Latin, French, English, English History, Chemistry, Mechanics and Mathematics. She later taught English and Religion at Howells School in Llandaff from 1908 to 1942, after which she retired aged 67 years. In her early years she could also be found preaching on a soapbox in Llandaff fields on a Sunday – it seemed to be the 'speakers' corner' of south Wales. She also had a stand at Cardiff Market from which she delivered impassioned speeches. She was an advocate of Pacifism and one National Eisteddfod submission compared her contribution to Pacifism alongside such iconic figures as Waldo Williams, Henry Richard, and R S Thomas. In 1948, in the *Hywelian Magazine*, an old pupil referred to the 'selfless devotion and unstinted energy she gave to the cause of World Peace... her determination never wavered, and she steadfastly upheld the ideals of the League of Nations, and preached her doctrine of pacifism on its highest level. She was indeed the stuff of which martyrs are made.'

Following her death in 1948, a letter from a local vicar to the *Western Mail* referred to her as 'one of the souls who gave herself without reserve to the cause of peace. The outbreak of the Second World War was a heavy blow to her, but she still laboured for the cause so near to her heart. Even when the bombs fell in Cardiff, she held fast to her faith in spite of many difficulties...'

A letter in the *Western Mail*, in February 1982, suggested she may have been an activist with *Peace News*, a pacifist magazine which was established in 1936 to serve the peace movement in the United Kingdom. Interestingly, *Peace News* had a large number of women contributors, including Vera Brittain, Rose Macauley, Ethel Thannin, Ruth Fry and Sybil Morrison, all leading pacifists of the era.

Ethel Maud must have been a remarkable person, upholding her pacifist beliefs over two world wars in a climate which was hostile to such a movement. Remarkably, she retained her position at Howells School throughout the Second World War when the school and its governors could have played the patriotic card and removed her. Ethel Maud also invested time in the University Settlement Movement in London. This movement encouraged university students to contribute to the development of the urban poor. Ironically, while Ethel Maud moved to London, a university settlement project was established in the East Moors area of Splott in Cardiff at the same time. During the First World War she enrolled as a member of the British Red Cross, from July 1914 until October 1918. She undertook nursing duties at Rookwood and St Fagans Hospital, Llandaff, for a total of 480 hours.

Talent also extended to the wider Bush family. William, James Bush's brother, was also a prominent educationalist and engineer. In 1874 he became the first headmaster of the Newport School of Arts and Science (later the Newport Technical Institute). Under his guidance, the school expanded and pupils excelled. Bush was a fellow of the Chemical Society and also a photographer, and was retained as a handwriting expert in the celebrated Parnell case (Pigott forgeries) and many other legal cases. He was adjudicator at the National Eisteddfod, a naturalist, and the winner of many national competitions in photography, maths and sciences. A very similar profile to James and, equally talented.

What a stimulating environment and family for young Percy Bush to be brought up in. A family at the leading edge of technical education, brothers making a living and excelling in arts and engineering across the United Kingdom and the Colonies, while Percy's mother and sister were fighting against traditional convention and prejudice.

Percy was christened Frank Percy Bush and was known to his family as Frank, but he was affectionately referred to as Percy from his early playing days. Building on this stimulating family life, Percy's education was spent at a small private school, St Mary's Hall (founded in 1880), situated in the centre of Cardiff. Percy was to be educated among contemporaries who went on to become leaders and influencers in Cardiff and the wider business community. They included Sven Hansen, Cardiff shipowner and director; Gilbert Shepherd, trustee of the *Times* and *Spectator* and head of the local Gilbert Shepherd Owen & Co. for many years; and W G Wiley, vice chairman of Reardon Smith Line. The school could also boast the fastest racing cyclist in Wales, Harry Prickett, among its former pupils and, of course, Percy Bush. The stimulating and challenging home environment was supported by a traditional Victorian / Edwardian private school education and, in later years, Percy and some of his contemporaries, particularly Gilbert Shepherd, would look back with fondness at the start St Mary's Hall had given them. The school also had rugby on the curriculum and its annual reports showed matches against a mixture of local schools, such as Richmond Road Juniors and Monkton House.

Reminiscing in 1948, Percy described how in a game versus Monkton House at the age of ten, St Mary's were leading by a try with a minute to go when Monkton House dropped a goal to win the game. This feat so impressed Percy that he became infatuated by the process of dropping goals and practised until the next game where St Mary's won by three drop goals to two converted tries. This early habit of dropping goals lasted throughout his playing career. He later went on to play for Penarth Collegiate School and for a local club in Canton (see Chapter 2).

James and Fanny Bush died within a day of each other in April 1923. Their obituary in the local *Evening Express* referred to their charming personalities which made them loved, and their work in education which earned them a place in Cardiff's annals. The obituary also highlights their role as parents to 'one of the finest rugby footballers the world has ever known'.

Percy inherited his confidence, sense of adventure, charm, and wit from his family, the period, and the city in which he grew up. Over the next few years his skills as a rugby player would be honed across a range of locations and countries, from the leafy suburbs of Canton and Llandaff in Cardiff, the university playing fields of Cardiff, the Rhondda Valley, Antipodean fields of Australia and New Zealand, the Arms Park, and Nantes in France. They all made their contribution in creating one of Wales' finest outside halves and rugby characters.

CHAPTER 2

Rugby from the Early Beginnings

PERCY WAS BORN in 1879 in Cardiff. Not only was the town a 'Klondike' for industrialists, shipowners, and colliery owners (who tended to reside in the town rather than in the coalfield areas), but it was also experiencing the impact of a new sport which had not only gripped the imagination of Cardiff, but other coastal towns and coalfield areas. As *Fields of Praise: The Official History of the Welsh Rugby Union, 1881–1981* illustrates, the arrival of rugby coincided with the greatest industrial expansion Wales had seen. Between 1880 and 1890, some 200,000 people moved into Glamorgan alone. The decade also saw the foundation of the Welsh Football Union, the forerunner of the WRU. 'South Wales in the late nineteenth century was a society where the sands were running in. It was a nervy society, but it was the nervousness that is the subtle complement to confidence.'

Cardiff Rugby Club was founded in 1876 and often drew between 3,000 and 4,000 spectators during the 1881/2 season, while a record crowd of 10,000 paid £500 to see Wales play Scotland in February 1890 at Cardiff. 'By the mid-1870s the rugby game was already moving out from the progressively minded schools to the wider community.'

Gwyn Prescott's recent analysis of the importance of rugby in Cardiff recorded an average of 200 teams playing in Cardiff between 1889/90 and 1896/7. Recreation and sport was particularly seen by the middle and upper class as a panacea for deteriorating morals, and for alleviating the poor social and difficult economic conditions which many of the working class in Cardiff and south Wales were experiencing.

The 'city fathers' were generous in laying out parks and gardens and Llandaff Fields were acquired in 1898, while Charles Thompson presented Thompson Park to the public of Canton as a playing field and gardens, enlarging them in 1895. They were conveniently situated opposite Percy's family home in Romilly Crescent.

The buzz associated with the emergence of rugby (as the leading team sport in south Wales), combined with his family background and the opportunities created by city fathers in terms of local recreation facilities, provided an ideal environment for the young Percy Bush to commence his career. The earliest records show Percy and his brother, Fred, playing in 1894/5 for a local team, Canton Crescents. No doubt the team was made up of pals who lived in the locality surrounding Romilly Crescent, a middle-class enclave situated in the emerging working-class community of Canton. A rugby team had existed in this part of Cardiff for some time which, as D H Lewis pointed out in his autobiography *America Made Me Welcome*, regularly provided players for Cardiff RFC, and he himself represented Cardiff and attained two caps in the 1885–88 seasons for Wales. Records show that the Canton Crescents played 21 matches in 1884/5 and were invincible, winning 17 and drawing 4 matches. Fourteen-year-old Percy occupied the left centre position, combining very effectively with his brother Fred to dominate the scoring. Fred was second top scorer with 19 tries, while Percy was top scorer with 14 drop goals and 16 tries – his penchant for drop goals already clearly evident. Apparently, according to a letter from a fan written in 1947, Percy had a particular style when looking to drop a goal, which involved him stubbing the toe of his right foot on his left leg stocking and then unleashing the drop goal.

The team went on to achieve further success locally when they entered a cup competition introduced by Cardiff RFC for under-16s and -17s team in 1896/7. As the Cardiff club history suggests: 'this was a practical gesture to stimulate the interest in local football.'

Sixteen teams entered the competition and the winners were Canton Crescents. Clearly the similarity between Canton Crescents and Romilly Crescents is not coincidental and perhaps reflects a desire by Percy and his pals to access the playing base of the expanding Canton area of the city. Reminiscing in 1948, Percy recalled his playing membership at the Canton Crescents. While Canton Crescents won the trophy in 1896/7, they lost the following year to St Peters seconds, 5–0. The competition clashed with those of the Cardiff and District Rugby Union and the Cardiff club handed it over to the new union. Canton Crescents were also participants in a nine-a-side tournament organised by the Cardiff club in 1896. They went on to beat St Andrews in the final, as the result of a goal kicked by a certain Winfield, who was probably the young H B Winfield of Cardiff and Wales from the first Golden Era. The games were played at Imperial Gardens, where the National Museum of Wales and Gorsedd Gardens are located today.

Percy's rugby education continued while he attended the newly formed University College, Cardiff, and he played for the university side between 1896 and 1899. It was while he was with the university team that both he and Fred came across Penygraig Rugby Club, a leading team in the Glamorgan league. Fred and Percy, in particular, went to play for the Valleys club between 1897 and 1900, with Percy captaining the team between 1898 and 1900. Fred played on the wing and Percy played in the centre. Together they were known as the 'two devils'. It is this connection with Penygraig which has led some commentators today to suggest that Percy was a product of the Rhondda Valley.

Percy and Fred travelled from Cardiff to the Rhondda by train to play for Penygraig. The Glamorgan league attracted large crowds and had a reputation not only of hard forward play but also short, sharp passing. What was the appeal to Percy of playing for a Valleys club?

Recalling his early career in 1948, Percy indicated that it was the university captain, W D Thomas, who persuaded him to play for Penygraig in 1897, as the result of a last-minute drop out. Percy played his first game at centre against Neath and had the 'pleasure' of playing against Bill James, a forward of 15 stones, picked to play in the centre against Percy.

Percy was warmly welcomed by the Penygraig supporters and players and was elected captain. Percy recalled that the role of captain terrified him because of the experience and age of the rest of the players, particularly the forwards. He thought he became a 'good captain – the best ever' because he was the only person who realised that his men 'knew a devil of a lot more about the game than he did himself – and let them do it'.

The journey to Penygraig and the 'frontier-like environment' and warmth associated with mining communities must have also provided a buzz of excitement for someone who had been brought up in a private school. There is no doubt that Percy's family believed in contributing their skills and abilities beyond the family, and young Percy was aware of the need to absorb and contribute fully to the changes taking place in industrial south Wales. (In 1908, several of the touring Australian team played for a Percy Bush XV versus Cardiff Roxboroughs, at the Arms Park, a game won by Bush's team, 31–3. The match was organised to raise funds for Christmas dinners for the poor of Cardiff.)

A press observer at a match between Cardiff and Penygraig at the Arms Park in January 1898 commented that, in respect of Percy and Fred Bush, 'They are not likely ever to become great... owing to lack of physical qualifications, but they showed some knowledge of the game'. Cardiff won the game, 30–0. The following year, Percy played his first game for the Cardiff first XV and received his reserves cap. Legend has it that it was Gwyn Nicholls who invited Percy to play for Cardiff, following one of the games versus Penygraig, and Percy made his Cardiff debut late in the 1900 season.

In Penygraig, Percy was a hero. His diminutive frame,

cast against the biggest and roughest Rhondda forward, certainly appealed to local spectators and club coaches.

A letter sent to Percy in 1938, from a former club member at Penygraig, highlights Percy's contribution and the warmth and affection shown to him during his period at Penygraig: 'I can remember you playing for dear old Penygraig and I for one know you did enjoy yourself amongst the old Bell Vue-Ites [the ground], idolised by these... you were no doubt the idol of the boys in those days, more so than was Billie Llewellyn in Lwynipia [*sic*]' (also a famous Welsh international).

The letter goes on to describe the playing conditions and refers to the legends of Rhondda and Wales forward play: 'Now be sporting Percy and tell the old and new what you felt like waiting to take a high punt such as Dick Hellings... George Kirkhouse, Harry Jones, Miller or Dai Evans would be pounding down upon you in those good old league days, no fun was it?' The author of the letter also refers to one of the first examples of Percy's famous ability to stop dead and sidestep, when he beat Dai Rees, the Treherbert full back, in the snow.

This and other letters sent to Percy also highlight the anguish of Penygraig supporters on hearing Percy had left the club to play for Cardiff, thus beginning a new and glorious chapter in his rugby career. He also played rugby for London Welsh RFC on occasions.

Outside of rugby, Percy was an accomplished soccer player and cricketer and played for the university, Cardiff Cricket Club, and had a few games for Glamorgan in the early part of the twentieth century. He was a right handed batsman. He played three Minor Counties Championship games against Wiltshire, Berkshire and Surrey seconds in the 1902/3 season. He represented the MCC on their tours to south Wales, and hit 41 against Glamorgan in July 1905 and 60 against Monmouthshire in July 1899, both matches won by the Welsh counties. But his career in rugby was just about to take off, not in Wales, but in Australia and New Zealand.

CHAPTER 3

With the Old Crocks in Australia and New Zealand, 1904

IN APPENDIX V of Clem Thomas' *The History of the British Lions*, published in 1996, only five players from outside the modern era, i.e. pre-1920, hold positions in the record tables: J F Byrne for his four conversions in the 1896 Test matches in South Africa, C Y Adamson for his ten points; A M Bucher for his two tries in the 1899 Test series against Australia; and Willie Llewellyn and Percy Bush of Wales, for their exploits on the 1904 tour to Australia and New Zealand. Bush holds the record for most dropped goals by a Lions player in Test matches – two, ahead of Barry John, Phil Bennett, and David Watkins. He also became the first player on a Lions tour to score 100 points.

There has been some debate as to whether the 1904 tour (and earlier ones) qualified as British Lions tours. Certainly, the 1904 team was the first to contain international players from all four home unions, as well as the standard non-international players. The invitation to tour was generally restricted to those who could afford time off from employment, and was limited primarily to professional men or men of independent means, as their daily allowance on tour was only two shillings (10p in today's money).

This tour was significant for its success in Australia, where it became the only British side to win all of its matches on a major visit. New Zealand was a different story, as the injuries piled up, and they lost their captain, Bedell-Sivright, after the opening game. They also lost the five Test matches there and finished with a playing record of, won 2, lost 2, drawn 1. Incidentally, they also lost a 'picnic game' against the Maoris at Rotorua, which has not been included in the official tour records.

The real impact of the 1904 tour for the Welsh was the fact that it was the first encounter with the New Zealanders – many of the New Zealand players would tour the United Kingdom, Ireland and France the following year. The tour not only established the size of the task in hand for the Welsh and the other home union players, but also introduced the skills and technique of the New Zealanders. It also allowed the Welsh players to develop tactics which would be used in the famous encounter in December 1905, utilising moves that found success in New Zealand, and playing on the expectations of the New Zealand players following their own detailed analysis of, in particular, Welsh back play.

The tour party consisted of 13 forwards, of whom there were only three internationals; and eight backs, of whom four were Welsh internationals. Percy Bush was uncapped. Incidentally, he started the tour weighing 10 stone 4 lbs and finished it heavier, at 11 stone 6 lbs, reflecting the tremendous hospitality afforded to the team on the tour. The 1904 touring team consisted of:

Full back	C F Stanger-Leathes	North Yorkshire & Northumberland
Three-quarters	J L Fisher	Hull & East Riding
	R T Gabe	Cardiff and Wales
	W F Jowett	Swansea and Wales
	W M Llewellyn	Newport and Wales
	P F McEvedy	Guy's Hospital
	E T Morgan (vice capt.)	Guy's Hospital, Kent and Wales
	A B O'Brien	Guy's Hospital and Kent
Halfbacks	P F Bush	Cardiff, Glamorgan
	F C Hulme	Birkenhead Park, Cheshire & England
	T H Vile	Newport and East Wales
Forwards	D R Bedell-Sivright (capt.)	Cambridge University & Scotland
	T S Bevan	Swansea and Wales
	S N Crowther	Lennox and Surrey
	D D Dobson	Oxford University, Devon and England
	R W Edwards	Malone, Belfast, Ulster and Ireland
	B F Massey	Yorkshire
	A F Harding	London Welsh, Cardiff and Wales
	C D Patterson	Malone
	R J Rogers	Weston Super Mare and Somerset
	S M Saunders	Guy's Hospital, Blackheath and Kent
	J T Sharland	Streatham and Surrey
	B I Swannell	Northampton, East Midlands
	D H Trail	Guy's Hospital, London Scottish & Surrey
Manager	A B O'Brien	Guy's Hospital and Kent

The invitation to tour had been received by players in the spring of 1904. The had been selected by a committee which consisted of, J Hammond, G H Harnett, G W McArthur and N Spicer. The party were to spend nine weeks in Australia and two weeks in New Zealand. The players travelled to Paris where they were entertained by the Stade Français club. They travelled south by train to Marseilles, where they joined the SS *Ormuz* for their five-week journey to Adelaide, thereon to Sydney, for the first game of the tour.

On their way, they stopped in Naples, and then travelled through the Suez Canal. Rhys Gabe, reminiscing in the 1940s, recalled the massive bunkers there full of south Wales coal. They also stopped in Colombo, then the capital of Ceylon (now Sri Lanka), where Gabe was duped while buying a dressing gown onshore. When it was delivered to the boat in a presentation box, Gabe was surprised to find the box empty. Soon after leaving Colombo, the team started to train before breakfast each morning. As training built up as they neared Australia, the tour party had a setback, losing their only ball in the Great Australian Bight.

As noted, the tour of Australia was a notable success, with all games won. However, for Percy Bush it was a triumph, as press reports indicated. He was a star on and off the field and Teddy Morgan, writing in 1921 in E H D Sewell's book, *Rugby Football Up To Date*, commentated: 'he was the only man who revelled on hard grounds [in Australia]. His famous sidestep and his wonderful drop kicking made him the outstanding man of the tour.' In Australia and New Zealand, Percy scored 100 points consisting of:

- 12 tries (top try scorer)
- 4 penalties
- 4 drop goals
- 4 field goals
- 10 conversions

For clarification, in 1904 a try and penalty were each valued at three points, while a drop goal and a field goal attracted four points each and a conversion two points. Arthur O'Brien was the second-highest points' scorer with one try and 17 conversions, giving a total of 37 points.

In total, 19 matches were played, excluding an unofficial 'picnic game' versus a Maori XV, which was lost, 8–6.

In terms of appearances, 'Boxer' Harding, the legendary Welsh forward, played in all 19 games. It was a tremendous performance and one which has not been beaten by subsequent British Lions teams to Australia and New Zealand. Following Harding was Bush and Crowther with 18 games, and O'Brien and Bevan with 17. Surprisingly, the captain Bedell-Sivright only played nine games on tour. Following his injury against Queensland early on in the tour, he played only two further games, one in New Zealand against Canterbury, and the last tour game against New South Wales. Press reports suggest that he played but had not fully recovered from his earlier knee injury. The players' appearance record was as follows:

Player	No. of Appearances
A F Harding	19
P F Bush	18
S N Crowther	18
A B O'Brien	17
T S Bevan	17
R T Gabe	16
D D Dobson	16
B I Swannell	16
T H Vile	15
W M Llewellyn	14
P F McEvedy	14
S M Saunders	13
R W Edwards	13
E T Morgan	13
D H Trail	12
C F Stanger-Leathes	11
D R Bedell-Sivright	9

R J Rogers	7
W F Jowett	6
F C Hulme	6
J T Sharland	6
J L Fisher	3
C D Patterson	3
B F Massey	3

The tour party, in terms of playing members, was miniscule compared to modern-day British Lions tours. More remarkably, only 16 players played more than ten games on the tour, with the remaining eight players playing between three and nine games each. Clearly, a large contingent of players were found wanting on the tour from a rugby-playing perspective. Excluding Bedell-Sivright and Hulme, who were injured, out of the six players who only played between three and nine games, one was an international, Jowett, and the others were uncapped.

In total, the side scored 54 tries, 5 penalties, 5 drop goals, 6 field goals and 33 conversions. Try scorers were:

Players	Number of tries
P F Bush	12
E T Morgan	7
W M Llewellyn	7
R T Gabe	5
D R Bedell-Sivright	5
T S Bevan	3
D D Dobson	2
W F Jowett	3
P F McEvedy	2
A B O'Brien	1
R W Edwards	1
C D Patterson	1

F C Hume	1
S N Crowther	1
T H Vile	1
B I Swannell	1
J L Fisher	1

Percy certainly hit Australia running, scoring a field goal and a try, while beating New South Wales, 27–0, in front of a 35,000 crowd at the Sydney Cricket Ground. The reaction of the local press was very positive (even for Australian press). 'Bush, in my opinion, outclassed for headiness, quite apart from individual effort, any other player I have seen in his position. Some of his feint dodging to the open side and then wheeling to the blind side, racing at his top in order to gain position for his inside centre Gabe – was excellent in itself.'

Later in life, Percy highlighted this game, particularly, for the warmth of the reception from the Sydney crowd. He was impressed by the reception from the Ladies Stand, which was a 'blaze of glory' and 'the variegated hues of their dresses, hats, and parasols (for brilliant sun shone late on a Spring day at home, with late Spring warmth in the air) made a picture which delighted us just as it revived us, like a cup of tea.' Percy described how throughout the rest of the ground a tremendous, long-drawn-out roar of heartening welcome greeted them, with waving of hats and brandishing of walking sticks, cheers and clapping from the men, and waving of hankies, gloves, parasols and cheers from the 'sweet things' in the segregated area.

The game against Bathurst at Western was won, 21–6. Percy kicked a conversion and a penalty goal. At the after-match function, Percy responded to the local mayor by making a humorous speech, while also advocating support for the Union game in its competition against Australia Rugby League and Rules.

In the second game against New South Wales, which resulted in a 29–6 victory, the local press, following Percy's three tries and a conversion, were incredulous that he had never represented Wales in an international contest. Sydney's *Daily Telegraph* referred to him as: 'part eel and part will-o'-the-wisp.'

The winning streak continued against Metropolitan without Bush, who missed the match (19–6), while the first Test was won against Australia at the Sydney Cricket Ground, 17–0, with Bush scoring a try and a dropped goal.

At this point in the tour, comparisons were being made to the 1903 New Zealand team, which also toured Australia. *The Observer*, a local newspaper, noted that the defence and pack may not have been strong enough to defeat New Zealand, yet the strength of the backs was acknowledged.

The undefeated record continued against Northern Districts, 17–3, and against Queensland, 24–5, with Bush making a major contribution in both games by scoring a try, conversion and penalty against Northern District, and a try and field goal against Queensland, who were known locally as 'Bannalanders'.

The winning sequence continued up to the second Test against Australia in Brisbane. Bush scored a conversion and a drop goal in the 17–3 victory over Metropolitan, and a try and a conversion in the 18–7 defeat of Queensland. Toowoomba were beaten 12–3 in a match which attracted a record crowd of 3,000 to the

Royal Agricultural Ground. In Brisbane, the Lions beat Australia 17–3 in a Test which attracted another record crowd of 16,000. Bush again dominated the game, scoring a try, drop goal, and a field goal.

The Observer remarked that 'Bush excelled both on and off the field. The life and soul of the British team is Percy F Bush... his saying and mannerisms are always quaint and entertaining and, while an artist out joking at the expense of his mates, he sometimes is the victim.'

The team moved to Armidale to play Northern Border, winning 26–9, with Bush top scoring with two penalties, one conversion and one try, before moving on to play Australia in Sydney in the third and final Test. The game was won 16–0, with Bush only contributing a conversion to the score. However, the *Sydney Sportsman* highlighted Bush's part in the victory: 'Bush was as good as ever and was about the best of the backs in attack. His tricky run towards the end of the game was a dandy.'

The Australian tour was a great success, particularly for Bush and the other Welsh backs. Gabe, Morgan and Llewellyn revelled playing on hard grounds and behind a pack in which Bedell-Sivright and Welsh forward, 'Boxer' Harding, excelled. However, the conclusion arrived at by press reports and observers alike was that the British Lions would need to improve their defence and forward play if they were to win against New Zealand during the next leg of the trip. At this stage they did not know that their 'robust' captain, Bedell-Sivright, would miss most of the remainder of the tour. The brilliance of the backs would be sorely tested by New Zealand teams with their own style of robust play and scientific rugby.

It was clear on arriving in New Zealand that the climate (30°F on arrival, compared to Brisbane where it had been 85°F in the shade), atmosphere and enthusiasm for the game were very different to that in Australia. In addition, the team would no longer be playing on hard grounds, and would have to adapt its style, particularly without its inspirational leader, Bedell-Sivright.

The press coverage was also at a different level to Australia. It was more technical, and involved detailed appraisals of players and tactics, which tended to concentrate on sensational aspects of the game and personalities. The British team had now entered a country where rugby was king and the crowd, press and players, exceptionally knowledgeable. The first match against Canterbury's rampaging pack, in the mud, snow and water of Lancaster Park, provided a stiff welcome to New Zealand. While the game was won by 5–3, with Bush converting Sivright's try, the injury to the captain, as noted, ruled him out of the rest of the tour.

While the local press recognised the cleverness of the British pack and the 'tricks' of the three-quarters, Bush was singled out for praise *and* criticism. Percy was recognised as both unpredictable and exciting in attack, but weak in defence. He was criticised for not 'going down' on the ball at the feet of Canterbury forward rushes. But 'when this player secures the ball, look out for the unexpected. You can't anticipate the man from Cardiff.'

The next game against Otago and Southland, played at Dunedin, was won, 14–8. On very slippery ground, Bush dropped a goal and scored a second try. The captain of Otago and Southland was W (Billy) Stead, who would be prominent as New Zealand vice captain on the 1905 tour to the UK.

Following the game some of the tour party appeared on stage in Dunedin before a packed audience to play a team of girls at netball, which the tourists won, 7–5. All part of a touring team's repertoire…

The team travelled by train, and at each stop large crowds gathered to cheer the tourists. At Palmerston, the train was held up so that the town council could present an address of welcome, and so that the brass band could render 'See the Conquering Hero Comes'!

At Timaru Oamaru, it was almost impossible to move in the crowd that had gathered on the platforms. The team eventually arrived in Wellington for the first Test.

Following a pattern, the three-quarters played well in attack and the forwards scrummaged well. However, the local newspaper was critical of its work in the loose and in defence. As for Percy, his drop goal was a remarkable effort. The press summarised him thus: 'Bush is a rugby freak. Meteor-like in attack, the man from Cardiff becomes a common squib in defence. If you were asked what one thought of Bush, one would reply, which one – the sparking player… or the Bush who turns his back on a forward rush…?'

Unlike Australia, teams in New Zealand did not fade in the second half of the game, which was when most of the games in Australia were won. The fitness of the New Zealand teams, and their great desire to win, was a feature of New Zealand rugby in 1904, as it has been for subsequent teams from that country.

The game against New Zealand at Athletic Park, Wellington, saw the first loss of tour, 9–3, with Harding kicking a penalty for the tourists in response to two tries. The most interesting aspect for the rugby historian is the review of the game which was included in the local newspapers by New Zealand skipper, Billy Stead. It reflects the level of analysis and thinking that New Zealand were putting into their rugby.

Stead believed that the British forwards lacked versatility in attack, while New Zealand had developed a strategy to address the counterattack of the British backs by encouraging:

> Our forwards, wings and halfbacks to backup when the backs were attacking, thus forming a line of defence behind the backs' attack. In defence there was then some provision that forwards and halves shoot out across and reinforce the backs.

In Britain the forwards' role was to scrum and win lineouts. In New Zealand, the forwards' role was being extended in defence and attack. In the same game, Percy and the Welsh Lions also came across Dave Gallaher, who would captain New Zealand on the 1905 United Kingdom and France tour. Gallaher spoiled attacks by disrupting Vile, the scrum half, and sometimes intercepted between Vile and Bush.

The British Lions were coming across tactics and personalities who would make a major impact on the 1905 tour. Just how much would the British team and, particularly, the Welsh squad members learn and absorb from the visit to New Zealand?

On the Monday following the game, the tourists travelled over 200 miles by train to play Taranaki. The train was held up and arrived close to midnight. The civic reception saw the team treated to a traditional Maori welcome. Rhys Gabe commented that it was such a thrilling experience that they forgot the lateness of the hour and the fatigue following their 17-hour journey and clamoured for encore after encore.

The game against Taranaki at New Plymouth was drawn, 0–0, with rain dominating proceedings, while the last official match in New Zealand, against Auckland at Alexandra Park, was lost, 13–0. The team travelled to Auckland by boat in a storm, and Rhys Gabe, looking back at the game, said that the team felt 'washed out' and this contributed to 'the worst game we played'. In the Auckland match, the play of Percy Bush was eagerly anticipated by the crowd. He put in some superb work in attack but the 'attention paid him by Gallaher and Nicholson took a lot of sting out of his play and he got few chances'.

Both Gallaher and Nicholson would resume battle with Percy and the Welsh contingent in the United Kingdom in 1905; Nicholson, particularly, in the game against Cardiff in which he scored a try due to an error by Percy.

Rhys Gabe, writing in 1946, suggested that the margin of defeat could have been greater, and highlighted the role played by Tommy Vile in bravely getting down to the Auckland forward rushes. The game also saw the tourists lose Rogers through injury, while O'Brien was partially incapacitated.

Having fulfilled their official commitments, the team headed for Rotorua for sightseeing, but accepted an invitation to play against a local Maori team at the request of the local chief. This was an unofficial game which they lost, 8–6. Referring to this game later in life, Rhys Gabe indicated that this was the toughest game he had ever played in, despite the Maoris playing without boots or stockings!

Returning to Sydney, the British team still had one engagement to fulfil against New South Wales, a game they won, 5–0. Percy Bush scored the try and kicked the conversion. The *Australian Star*, in summarising the tour, indicated: 'Bush the... Welsh half, stood out from all his comrades as an attacker. On occasions his play was electric. He evaded his opponents in astonishing style, always ran ahead and if surrounded occasionally drop kicked a goal from difficult angles. He was undoubtedly the scoring machine of the team.'

Bush and the rest of the Welsh backs left Australia and New Zealand with reputations enhanced, particularly Bush, as the only non-international. Bush also established a style of exciting, scintillating running and superb kicking, alongside a less than confident defence – a combination which would dominate the debate about his merits for the rest of his career.

He returned to Cardiff to be greeted by 1,000 club members. The long return journey across the Pacific to Vancouver on the SS *Aorangi* included stops at Suva, Samoa and Honolulu. From Vancouver they crossed the Rocky Mountains to Winnipeg and Fort William, crossing Lake Superior by steamer. They then travelled by train to Toronto and New York and returned to Liverpool aboard the SS *Carpania*. Views of the tour were exchanged. Although they ended the tour disappointed, they were well prepared for the visit of the 1905 New Zealand team, having absorbed a number of lessons.

Rhys Gabe, quoted in the New Zealand press following the Test defeat, was confident that a Welsh team could indeed beat New Zealand.

The style and play of Bush, and his identification by New Zealand as a potential match winner, would be fully utilised in the most celebrated international game of rugby of all time.

Percy's first team, Cardiff Crescents, 1894–5. Percy is sitting on the far left in the second row.

East Wales team assembled for their trial game versus West Wales, Easter 1905. This match was in preparation for the visit of the All Blacks.

Wallace, a member of the All Blacks team, practising kicking before meeting Wales.

Those Terrible "All Blacks."

"Your turn next old chappie."

New Zealand followed up their famous victory over Scotland by defeating Ireland last Saturday, and this week England will be called upon to face the music.

New Zealand v. Wales.

Dame WALES: "I expect it do smart a bit, but there's determined I was not to let you have things all your own way <u>here</u> like you have elsewhere."

THURSDAY, DECEMBER 21st, 1905.

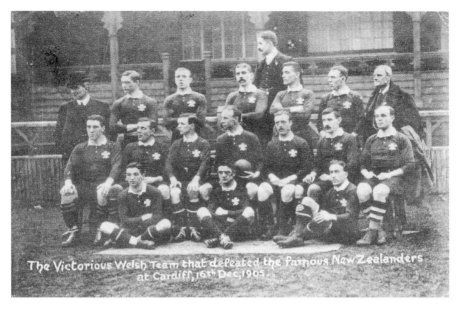

The victorious Wales team that defeated New Zealand in 1905.

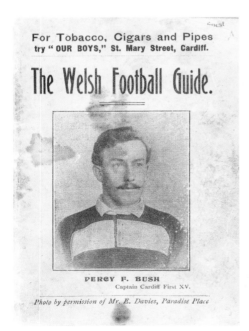

Welsh football guide, 1905.

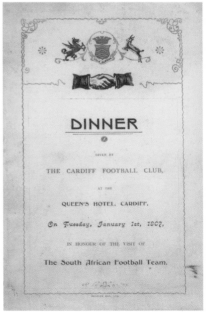

Dinner menu after the Cardiff RFC versus South Africa match, 1907.

Left: Series of cartoons capturing the interest and emotion surrounding the 1905 game against New Zealand.

Action postcard from the Cardiff RFC versus South Africa game, 1907.

Percy Bush ready to receive a ball from the scrum during the Cork Constitution versus Cardiff match in 1907.

Programme for Cardiff RFC versus South Africa, 1907.

Cardiff RFC team photograph versus South Africa, 1907.

Cardiff RFC team versus Australia, 1908.

BACK ROW—T. S. Griffen, W. S. Prentice, D. B. Carroll, A. J. McCabe, J. Stephenson, P. Carmichael.
SECOND ROW—S. M. Wickham, P. Flanagan, C. McMurtrie, P. Burge, P. A. McCue, S. A. Middleton, F. B. Smith, T. Richards, N. E. Row,
R. R. Craig.
THIRD ROW—E. Parkinson, C. H. McKivatt, E. Mandible, E. McIntyre, Dr. H. M. Moran (Capt.), Captain J. McMahon (Manager),
F. Wood (Vice-Capt.), J. T. Barnett, C. A. Hammond, C. Russell.
BOTTOM ROW—J. Hickey, M. McArthur, W. Dix, H. Daly.
K. A. Gavan.   A. B. Burge.
Photo by R. Scott & Co.}   COPYRIGHT |Manchester

Australia touring team versus Cardiff RFC, 1908.

The Victorious Welsh Team, 1908,

Who defeated Scotland at Swansea, February 1st, 1908.

The most exciting and interesting International Match ever witnessed.

COPYRIGHT PHOTOGRAPH.   W. H. STEPHENS, ATHLETIC PHOTOGRAPHER.
                                                                           NEWPORT, MON.

Mr. JARRETT.   W. NEILL.   J. WEBB.   J. BROWN.   W. H. DOWELL.   G. HAYWARD.   J. WATTS.   Mr. ACK LLEWELLYN
(W.F.U.)   (W.F.U.)
    W. TREW.   R. A. GIBBS.   H. B. WINFIELD.   G. TRAVERS   R. T. GABE.   J. WILLIAMS.   A. F. HARDING.
                                              (Captain).
                        T. H. VILE.   P. F. BUSH.

Wales team versus Scotland at St Helen's, Swansea, 1908.

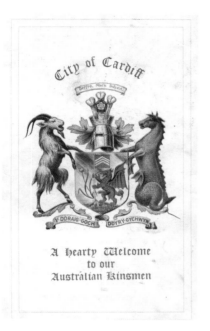

Menu for Cardiff RFC versus Australia, 1908.

Programme for Cardiff RFC versus Australia, 1908.

Percy Bush and Tommy Vile, selected to play together versus Scotland in 1908.

Crowd scenes at Cardiff Arms Park. Note the ladies' interest in the game.

CHAPTER 4

International Player

WHILE BUSH EMERGED from the tour to Australia and New Zealand with his reputation sky-high and the subject of lavish press reports, he was not guaranteed his international place.

Rugby writer J B G Thomas summarised the attributes of Percy well, and perhaps highlighted in a nutshell some of the reasons why he only played on eight occasions for Wales:

> ...his puckish sense of humour, his love of the practical joke, especially at the expense of administrators and the fact he played the game for fun, however cleverly, produced much criticism of his play, but he was a great one, even if he was the 'wickedest' and most confident of them all.

Commentators at the time highlighted his 'sense of fun', 'practical joke playing', 'his supreme confidence' and perhaps 'arrogance', along with his ability to wind up both players and administrators. As such, he was a unique individual who administrators particularly found difficult to control.

Townsend Collins, who saw Percy play and was very much a part of the Welsh rugby scene during the first Golden Era, was unusually blunt in suggesting, 'he was not greatly liked by the Welsh Union'. Press reports following the second Welsh trial in 1905 suggested that Bush 'has won his way against all prejudices'. Interestingly, he was one of the very few Cardiff players of his era who did not represent the Barbarians, yet he appeared to have all the necessary qualities required by that special club.

While some administrators may have disliked Percy, 'his players worshipped him', as can be seen from correspondence in later years with his fellow players and supporters, and from 'reviews' held for him on his brief return visits to Cardiff from France in the 1930s.

His international career saw him play on eight occasions (with only one defeat) for Wales, as follows:

1905	New Zealand at Cardiff	(won)	3–0
1906	England at Richmond	(won)	16–3
1907	South Africa at Swansea	(lost)	11–0
	Ireland at Cardiff	(won)	29–0
1908	England at Bristol	(won)	28–18
	Scotland at Swansea	(won)	6–5
1910	Scotland at Cardiff	(won)	14–0
	Ireland at Dublin	(won)	19–3

In total Percy scored two tries, three drop goals, and a conversion. His first try came on what was probably, apart from the famous 1905 game, his greatest performance for Wales, against Ireland in 1907 in Cardiff, where he was a replacement for Billy Trew who dropped out prior to the game. His second try was scored against England in 1908, at the famous 'phantom football match', played in thick fog at the Bristol City AFC ground at Ashton Gate.

In terms of halfback partners, Percy played with Dicky

Owen of Swansea in the first three of the eight games (versus New Zealand, England and South Africa). In the 1907 game against Ireland, he was partnered by his Cardiff scrum half Dicky David, the window cleaner from Canton. In the remaining games (England and Scotland in 1908 and Ireland in 1910), his great friend and confidant, Tommy Vile of Newport, his Lions scrum half, wore the number nine shirt. Against Scotland in 1910, following Dicky David's departure to rugby league, W L Morgan (Teddy Morgan's brother) of Cardiff was selected to partner Percy at scrum half.

There has been considerable speculation regarding the partnership of Dicky Owen and Percy Bush. While they played well together, it was felt by many commentators that Owen would not play with Bush if he could help it, yet would not give way to Vile unless injured. J B G Thomas puts this down to the 'East v West' rivalry.

Certainly the selectors (under pressure from the more established Owen) seemed to prefer club halfbacks and, with Owen from Swansea, the fly half berth was more often than not filled by Swansea players, such as Jones and Bancroft. However, it is clear from contemporary reports that both Owen and Bush were very different characters. 'Bush was as wicked off the field as was Owen on it.' Percy's puckish sense of humour and overpowering personality was in great contrast to Dicky Owen.

Owen was a rugby genius and a great tactician and he may have decided that the risk associated with playing with Bush may have been too great, and he preferred to have himself as the master tactician and not leave the outcome of the game to a 'wayward rugby genius'. Or it may be, as J B G hinted, just a clash of backgrounds;

Owen was a working man and Percy was a professional man. However, writing in 1948, Rhys Gabe commented that while both Percy and Dicky Owen were geniuses in their respective positions, they could never blend with each other on the three occasions they played together for Wales. Gabe highlights that Owen suited the style of play of Dick Jones and Billy Trew admirably (both Swansea outside halves) but 'he wouldn't do what Percy wanted, and that was to throw the ball out as soon as he got it'. If he had, Gabe believed, it would have cramped Owen's style considerably.

The halfbacks preferred by Percy were Dicky David, Tommy Vile and Billy Morgan 'for then he had plenty of time to concoct his cunning strategy'. Gabe comments that Percy would have loved to have combined with Haydn Tanner because of his 'bullet-like passes'. Percy, reminiscing in the 1940s on the 1907 game versus Ireland, emphasised that he enjoyed playing with Dicky David because 'he was content to be an inside half, and from who I could therefore expect to see the ball now and again', clearly a swipe at Owen's style of play.

The pressures to use club partners, and the rivalry between combinations from East and West Wales, was reflected in the selection of the Welsh team to meet Scotland in 1909. Percy injured his back and finger in a club game and was forced to step down. Press reports indicated that, owing to Percy's 'defection', Tommy Vile stood down as well. Jones and Dicky Owen of Swansea replaced the East Wales pair.

Rugby supporters and the ladies from across south Wales adored Percy. The *South Wales Graphic*, a magazine for the local Edwardian Society, in 1905, described him as the 'most popular halfback in the Kingdom'.

What other international player or club captain at that time would have the audacity and confidence to escort his fiancée across the Arms Park just before the kick-off at every Cardiff home game, from the north-west corner of the then club ground to the front row seats in the old stand (south side of the old Arms Park) before returning to lead the teams on to the field?

What other player would have the unbridled cheek to challenge the 1908 Australian side prior to their game with his Cardiff team, with a sword and shield (relics from Rorke's Drift), as a counter to their 'war dance'?

In those days the local press and supporters, particularly in west and east Wales, were great advocates of their own men, and certainly Bush and Vile were heavily criticised by the west Wales press despite the win over Scotland at Swansea in 1908. So much so that press reports in the east of Wales were quick to address the criticism and, in return, question the impartiality of the Swansea press who, 'judging from their comments know as much of the matters of impartiality and fairness as mules know of astronomy. No fault can be found by the Swansea fold of the play of international men from their district.'

The press reports from the game maintain that Bush was 'clean off his game' and was closely managed by his opposing centre. However, Scottish critics still pointed out that it was Bush, more than anyone else, who preserved Wales' record.

The 'tension' between east and west Wales over selection, and Percy Bush in particular, was vividly reported in the *London Evening Standard* prior to the Wales game against Scotland in Cardiff in 1910.

Commenting on notes received from a 'well-known Welsh critic', the article cites the rivalry between each town as a cause of the tension, and highlights the supporters of Neath who had heartily hooted the defeated Welsh team following a victory by England, partly because it had no Neath representation.

With reference to Percy ('the versatile but woefully erratic Cardiff player') the Welsh critic suggests his selection was a surprise. The critic quotes: 'At his best, Bush is unbeatable; at his worst, he is impossible.' The article goes on to criticise Bush's tackling but then suggests: 'Really, Bush will have much to do with the making or breaking of Wales.' The article goes on to suggest that the selection of the two Cardiff players, Morgan at scrum half and Spiller at centre, was just to help Bush.

The critic goes on to expose his allegiances when he suggests that the centre, Billy Trew of Swansea, 'a safe fielder', will be troubled by Bush's ridiculous system of passing. Further exposing his team preferences, the critic goes on to undermine Morgan, the Cardiff scrum half, by reminding the readers he is related to the famous Dr Teddy Morgan, and refers to him as a mechanical scrum half, not in the same class as Dicky Owen of Swansea. To ram his point home further, the critic reminds everyone that: 'Bush has always failed in partnership with R M Owen.'

The rugby reporter of the *Standard* reminds his readers how very seriously Welsh people take the build-up to an international match, while distancing himself from the 'doubts' raised by the critic. Wales won the game, 14–0, with Billy Spiller of Cardiff scoring a sparkling try on his debut.

The international game versus South Africa at Swansea in 1906, was the only international game Bush played in and lost. The defeat, 12–0, was a great shock and certainly Bush and Nicholls were heavily criticised. One spectator writing to Percy in 1947 indicated that 'you and Dicky Owen did not function as I expected'. The press criticism stung Bush and Nicholls and they resolved to revenge their and Wales' reputation when South Africa met Cardiff later in the tour.

At international level there is no doubt that outside the famous 1905 Test versus New Zealand, Bush's greatest games for Wales were against Ireland in 1907 and England in 1908.

The match at Cardiff versus Ireland was referred to by Townsend Collins as 'Bush's match'. 'Rarely has a game been so dominated by the performance of one man.' Both he and his Cardiff club mate, Dicky David, showed perfect understanding which led to many commentators advocating the selection of club pairs more frequently for Wales. Bush destroyed the Ireland team single-handed, 'with a brilliant run he beat half a dozen men and then from a scrum David sent the ball back to Bush and he dropped a goal'. Later in the game, 'Bush went through with a brilliant run, Maclear [the great Irish international] flung himself at the place where the Cardiff man's leg had been, but by that time his body was somewhere else'. Townsend, an eyewitness, suggested that 'throughout the game he was pivot of the attack, audacious, confident, supreme in skill'.

Looking back later in life, Percy described it as a match to remember, not only for his performance but for other factors too. It was his pal, Rusty (Rhys) Gabe's first match as captain and he was also partnered by his old Cardiff scrum half, Dicky David. Prior to the game, Percy had been confined to bed with quinsy and could only train by running up and down the stairs. To explain his absence from training sessions, he had let it be known that he was 'preparing by taking the waters at Llandrindod Wells'. Dicky David called at Percy's house every day prior to the game, as it was his first cap. He knew that if Percy dropped out, the Union would drop him and insert another club halfback pair.

Against England at Bristol, the fog descended and Bush, on and off the field, was his 'impish' best. Prior to the game he informed the press that 'Wales would be playing with the fog'. In the game he dropped a goal and made a try for his club colleague and friend, Rhys Gabe. At half-time, he was found in the crowd chatting away to supporters. Bush was to play twice more for Wales, in 1910.

While Bush was restricted to eight international caps, his international career will always be linked to the famous 1905 game versus New Zealand. Much has been written about the game, and I do not wish to go over too much old ground again in this book, but rather bring together some new eyewitness accounts.

My contention, however, is that the winning score owed a lot to the new scientific thinking and planning which was apparent in the Welsh game at the time. It was based on a pre-planned move which believed that New Zealand would pay particular attention to Bush and the backs who had toured New Zealand in 1904, particularly the well-documented tactic of Bush using the blind side effectively.

All major battles are won with meticulous planning and the 1905 game was one of the finest examples of the Welsh adopting a brand of forward thinking that was sometimes criticised in England and Scotland for being too professional an approach to the game.

The 1905 tour by the New Zealand team had been officially announced on 23 June 1904. The decision by the Welsh Union to hold trials at Easter 1905 in Cardiff between East and West Wales was part of the preparation. The game attracted one of the biggest ever crowds seen for a non-international game, 30,000, with gate receipts of £500, a record then for such a match. In all, the trial included 11 players who would eventually play against the New Zealanders in December 1905. The teams were as follows:

East		
Full back	D J Boots	Newport
Backs	E G Nicholls	Cardiff (capt.)
	R T Gabe	Cardiff
	W Llewellyn	Newport
	E T Morgan	London Welsh
Halfbacks	P F Bush	Cardiff
	T H Vile	Newport
Forwards	A Brice	Cardiff
	A F Harding	London Welsh
	J Hodges	Newport
	G Boots	Newport
	W Neill	Cardiff
	E Thomas	Newport
	P Shugar	Penygraig
	D Jones	Aberdare

West

Full back	G Davies	Swansea
Backs	D Rees	Swansea (capt.)
	W Trew	Swansea
	G Arnold	Swansea
	W Arnold	Swansea
Halfbacks	R Jones	Swansea
	D Owen	Swansea
Forwards	W Joseph	Swansea
	F Scrines	Swansea
	S Bevan	Swansea
	D Thomas	Swansea
	D Davies	Swansea
	H Watkins	Llanelli
	G Vicory	Aberavon
	D Fryer	Mountain Ash

East Wales played in blue and black and West Wales in white. The *Western Mail* described the great excitement surrounding the game, with thousands of enthusiasts from all parts of south Wales flocking to the game and spending the morning and early afternoon 'doing the sights of the town' and 'discussing the prospects of victory for either of the two sides'. East Wales won the game, 18–4, with the *Western Mail* reporter indicating that the West Wales team were well beaten and 'without paying regard to past little differences of opinions they will, I am certain, readily agree with what I have consistently upheld in the face of much cheap ridicule that Bush is a great player'.

The reporter went on to emphasise (with an eye on readers from west Wales and the selectors) how Bush and Vile could be trusted anywhere, and also highlighted the performance of Dai Jones, George Boots and Will Joseph. All of whom, except Vile, got the selectors' vote for the game against the All Blacks the following December.

However, while much of the credit for planning the move which created Teddy Morgan's famous try was laid at the feet of the great general, Dicky Owen of Swansea, it is important to highlight the role of Percy Bush as a decoy runner to the blind side move. This gave the opportunity for Dicky Owen to attack the blind side of the scrummage on the right, with Bush and Llewellyn outside him, and then change direction to the left, before passing to Pritchard, who passed to Gabe and then on to Teddy Morgan who ran in for a try from 20 yards out. The clash of personality between Bush and Owen, and Owen's preference to play with his Swansea colleagues, has already been discussed. Perhaps, on this occasion, Owen, in discussion with the 1904 tourists, recognised the importance of Bush in the plan to deceive the New Zealanders and hence his willingness to support Bush's selection in the big game. Could the seeds of this move have been planted on board the *Aorangi* on the return trip from New Zealand by the Welsh representatives of the returning British touring team?

Certainly, Bush's habit of feinting open side and then accelerating blind was well documented on the tour, and both the Australians and New Zealanders had targeted Bush as one of the most dangerous members of the team who scored a number of his tries on the blind side. In the second Test versus Australia, the press commented that: 'Bush fooled the opposition with brilliant dodging and scored on the blind side of the scrum.'

Following the first Test against New Zealand at Wellington, in front of 30,000 spectators, the *New*

Zealand Times highlighted the struggle between the New Zealand forwards and the British backs, 'and one move stood out in strong relief from all others, the little Welshman P Bush. Whenever the ball reached him... there would be a rush of New Zealand forwards to fall upon him, lest he might by his lightning drop kicks, turn his side's probable defeat into victory ... Of the four players in the three-quarters of Great Britain, three were Welshmen and all these were good.'

These three Welshmen went on to play in the 1905 Test in Cardiff.

With the New Zealanders appetite for detailed analysis now well known to the Welsh players on tour, there is little doubt that, in the planning for the 1905 Test, Wales were going to give the New Zealanders exactly what they were anticipating, a blind-side run from Bush. The rest is history.

CHAPTER 5

The Rugby Championship of the World

THE 1905 GAME against New Zealand is probably one of the most talked about internationals of all time. Even though the game was played 110 years ago, it still is the subject of intense analysis and controversy. Why is this? The dispute surrounding Deans' try, still a sore point for many New Zealanders today, is one obvious reason. Huw Richards describes the controversy as 'rugby's equivalent of Geoff Hurst's second goal in the 1966 World Cup [final], debated ever since...' Did Deans score or was he held back? Was the referee slow to arrive to see the Welsh players pull him back on the line? Why, if Deans scored, did he try to wriggle forward, as claimed by the Welsh tacklers?

This analysis will produce new independent third-party evidence – in writing – which claims Deans did not score. More of that later.

The 1905 international also brought together two unbeaten teams. New Zealand, who had carried all before them, were matched up against a Welsh team unbeaten at home since 1899, 'whose strategy was to attack and were not in awe of the All Blacks machine'.

The *Western Mail* described it as the 'Rugby

Championship of the World', which captured the imagination of the rugby-playing world and press. The British press, following the failure of sides to overcome or even get close to the colonials, also saw the game as the last opportunity to demonstrate 'that it is not yet time for relegating the old country to a museum as a crusted antiquity'.

Following the New Zealanders crushing of the best teams in England and Scotland, it was left to 'Gallant Little Wales' to defend the honour of the mother country. Wales took up the challenge, and it was also an opportunity for Wales to define itself as a nation. Following the victory, the local press had little difficulty in reminding the rugby world that Wales had triumphed where the Saxons had failed.

The local newspapers were intent on covering every aspect of the tour and, from early December, following the successful progress of the New Zealanders, the press fed on the intense interest from the Welsh public and the detailed preparations being made by the Welsh Football Union to ensure a successful game and outcome. It is as if the Union realised at an early date that the eyes of the rugby-playing world and media would be focused on Cardiff on 18 December for the unofficial world championship of rugby.

In late November 1905, an advert in the *Cardiff Evening News* offered two grandstand tickets for the match for £2 each (£206 in today's prices). Their face value was just five shillings. The demand for tickets was such that the police, with the Welsh Football Union, announced that forged tickets were in circulation. The local press also carried the debate about who would referee the game, suggesting on 5 December that Charles O'Neill, from Ireland, would officiate. A follow-up story, on 8 December, suggested that the All Blacks had nominated Robin Wales of Scotland, preferring him to O'Neill.

As early as 4 December, the local press indicated that excursions were being run to Cardiff for the great match from London, Manchester, Liverpool, Birmingham, Weymouth, Torquay, Cheltenham, Glasgow and Bristol, and one from Cork, Ireland, via New Milford (Neyland), all keen to see two unbeaten teams.

The All Blacks arrived in Cardiff on 8 December to a great reception and resided at the Queen's Hotel. The local press suggested that, after a few days in Wales, the All Blacks appeared to have lost a great deal of confidence, inferring that the 'football atmosphere' did not seem to agree with them. The All Blacks admitted that they had not 'breathed' anything like this in any other part of the kingdom. The New Zealanders were entertained regally and visited the Port of Cardiff, where they likened the local coal trimmers to 'All Blacks'. On 15 December they met the Lord Mayor and Corporation of Cardiff, when they were presented a gold medal pendant consisting of the Cardiff arms, red dragon and silver fern on a medal by the Lady Mayoress.

There was intense speculation in the press of the make-up of the Welsh team, following the two trials. There was also conjecture concerning the style of play. The press believed that the Welsh Football Union was determined to follow other countries in adapting the New Zealand style in preference to their own, as evidenced by the Probables team having seven forwards and eight backs. Following the second trial, the local press, in anticipating the final team, boldly announced that, 'Percy Bush has won his way against all prejudices'. They also suggested that, on the basis of the trial, J F Williams and J C Jenkins would replace Dai Tarw Jones and Harry Wetter who were relegated to the Possibles. The press were wrong and, out of the Possibles pack, Jehoida Hodges and Dai Tarw Jones were eventually selected for the 1905 game. Hodges' selection was a surprise to some, as he was 'crocked' for most of the season.

Critics, particularly in the English press, believed the style of play would not disrupt New Zealand, particularly in scrummaging, while the recall of veterans and crocks would favour New Zealand. Eager to improve their combinations, the whole Welsh back line (except Dicky Owen) played for Cardiff against Blackheath in London on 9 December.

Wales, like New Zealand, were at the forefront of 'scientific rugby' and the Union and players had been preparing for this game since June 1904 – nothing was left to chance. The marketing and organisation of the game, and the build-up musical selection was planned in advance to give Wales the greatest chance of victory.

Morning of the Game

The *Daily Mail*'s correspondent reported that as early as 9 a.m. excited supporters, some of whom had travelled all night from remote colliery districts, clamoured for admission to the ground. A local newspaper highlighted how a large number of men, on strike at Risca in Monmouthshire, had walked all the way to Cardiff (a distance of 16 miles) to see the game.

Because of the number of supporters outside the

ground clamouring for the best view of the game, the police, in discussion with the Union, opened the gates at 10 a.m. and by noon the *Daily Mail* reported that there was scarcely standing room left.

With interest in the game at fever pitch, the *Western Mail*'s rugby correspondent, 'Forward', was concerned that the packed mass on the shilling stand was swaying dangerously, two hours before kick-off (a feature of the great stadium for the next 80 years). The crowd was reported to be good tempered, however, and was eager to join in with the band in rendering the popular music of the times. At this time of the day, the *Western Mail* reports that the weather was fine: 'there was scarcely a breath of wind and the light was perfect.'

The grandstand was filling up and contained a section of ladies who had taken advantage of the fine weather to 'don their multi-coloured garments'. This would not have been an unusual sight at a big game in 1905, when leading clubs like Cardiff had actively embraced the demands of Edwardian ladies and issued special 'ladies tickets'.

The *Daily Mail*'s correspondent, unlike his equivalent from the *Western Mail*, appeared enthralled with the atmosphere from an early stage and devotes large parts of his report to the crowd and also to the singing prior to the game. He commented:

> ... from the crowd arose a continuous crucible of ardent Celtic chatter, broken by the deep harmonious resonance of some patriotic refrain started by a small knot here and there, was caught up on either side until the whole ground became enveloped in a noble volume of sound, perfect in rhythm and feeling, as from some 40,000 trained choristers led by some invisible master baton.

The *Daily Mail*'s correspondent quotes an English international at the game:

> I don't think there's any team in the world selected from all over the British Empire, that could beat Wales at Cardiff... Celtic electricity in the air... Loosens our sinews and weakens our joints and has a marvellously astringent effect on the home team!

There is no doubt that the selection of songs and hymns prior to kick-off was designed to 'awaken patriotic fervour' through the playing of 'Men of Harlech', 'Ar Hyd y Nos', and then 'Captain Morgan's March' with the following stirring lines, 'Men of Morganwg, rise against the foe! Send him hence or lay him low ... Morgan calls you, bids you with him stand. Drive the raiding Saxon from this fair land.'

Imagine how the New Zealand team, changing in the adjoining Cardiff pavilion, must have felt on hearing this outpouring of Celtic emotion and fervour up to two hours before the game. This indeed was like no other game they had played in or location visited. The New Zealanders were playing the whole country, not just fifteen players. All of Wales, through the crowd's passion and zeal, would be at Cardiff Arms Park.

About twenty minutes before kick-off, a thick mist hung over the ground and dimmed the light. The *Western Mail* reported that the crowd seemed to improve its temper and sung with great gusto traditional tunes such as, 'The Old Brigade', 'Tôn-y-Botel' (Ebenezer) and John Henry Newman's hymn, 'Lead, kindly light'.

It is worth recalling the words to this latter popular hymn of the day because it was sung by Edwardians and Victorians at times of danger or tragedy to inspire the congregation and to put their trust in God to lead them on and, like 'Cwm Rhondda' (not yet widely used until 1907), encourage supporters in pleading for divine support and intervention:

> Lead, kindly light, amid the encircling gloom,
> Lead thou me on;
> The night is dark, and I am far from home;
> Lead thou me on;
> Keep thou my feet; I do not ask to see
> The distance scene: one step enough for me.

Similarly 'The Old Brigade', a slow march written in 1881, also had lyrics to help raise the passion of the crowd and inspire the team: 'Where are the boys of the Old Brigade / Who fought with us side by side / Shoulder to shoulder, and blade by blade / Fought till they fell and died!'

What stands out about the song selection prior to the match is how inclusive it was, combining traditional songs, popular tunes of the day, Nonconformist hymns and hymns to engage the Established Churchgoers and the high church / Catholics – a song for everyone in the crowd of 40,000. Of course, with chapel and church attendance still high in 1905, the whole crowd would know the hymns and lyrics and be able to relate them to the context of the game. A great deal of thought and consideration was placed in the hymn and song selection, all part of the plan to beat New Zealand. As the pre-match singing continued, the *Western Mail* detected increasing tension in the crowd:

Beneath the outward merriment there run an under-current of intense suppressed excitement and it was time now when the prospects of the match were discussed with bated breath.

Outside the ground, it was chaotic, with the gates closed and thousands clamouring for a view of the game. The Devonport and Torquay excursion train for the great match arrived after the gates were closed. Anxious to view the game after a long journey, three to five shillings were paid by the passengers to stand on the roof of hansom cabs in Westgate Street to obtain a glimpse of the game.

The Game

Gallaher led the All Blacks on to the Arms Park and Gwyn Nicholls followed with the Welsh team. The teams were as follows:

Wales	New Zealand
H B Winfield (Cardiff)	G A Gillett (Canterbury)
W M Llewellyn (Penygraig)	D McGregor (Wellington)
E Gwyn Nicholls (capt.) (Cardiff)	R G Deans (Canterbury)
R T Gabe (Cardiff)	W J Wallace (Wellington)
T Morgan (London Welsh)	J Hunter (Taranaki)
C C Pritchard (Pontypool)	H J Mynott (Taranaki)
P F Bush (Cardiff)	F Roberts (Wellington)
R M Owen (Swansea)	D Gallaher (capt.) (Auckland)
W Joseph (Swansea)	G Tyler Auckland)
G Travers (Pill Harriers)	S Casey (Otago)
J J Hodges (Newport)	F Newton (Canterbury)
C M Pritchard (Newport)	F Glasgow (Taranaki)
D Jones (Aberdare)	J O'Sullivan (Taranaki)
A F Harding (London Welsh)	A McDonald (Otago)
J F Williams (London Welsh)	C Seeling (Auckland)

Following the Haka, the Welsh team sang 'Hen Wlad Fy Nhadau' led by Willie Llewellyn, and the crowd joined in producing an immense volume of sound. The *Daily Mail* reporter appeared overawed. 'There was a semi religious, almost fanatical invocation in the fervour when the great assembly took up the strain, "The Land of My Fathers! The Land of the Free!"'

Throughout his account of the game, the correspondent continually referred to the influence of the crowd, and the result, commenting that the 'All Blacks on Saturday seemed to be labouring under some strange hypnotic influence from the moment they stepped onto the field'. Other independent observers at the game, and the All Blacks captain himself, also suggested that the crowd had an effect on the outcome of the game.

Englishman Trevor Wignall, a celebrated sports writer, in an article for the *Strand Magazine* in 1944, was asked to identify which sporting event had surpassed all others in terms of the thrill it provided and which still left the clearest memories. He cited the 1905 game as the number one event, forty years later. He was in his seat before the game. He described how the New Zealanders' war cry led to a hush that fell on the crowd:

> It was as though something damp and dismal had settled on the watching rows of faces, destroying the spirit behind them. Then, from somewhere near a touchline, a man wearing a bowler hat and carrying a great leek, stepped on the field. For a few seconds he held the leek aloft, then he dropped it in a down-beat. Instantly, the whole gathering sung and swept into the strains of the National Anthem.

Wignall went on to describe the singing as, not so

much melody, but a combined call, prayer, command. It uplifted the Welsh players as much as it did the onlookers. Dave Gallaher, the New Zealand captain, told Wignall in an interview after the game that 'the singing had more to do with the defeat of his side than anything else that happened'. Gallaher said that midway into the game he wanted to 'kneel down and close his eyes'.

Wignall also claimed it was not only the greatest football game he had ever seen, but it was the greatest, most pulsating spectacular that he had ever attended. An amazing statement from a man who had witnessed many of the great global sporting events up to the Second World War.

An eyewitness, in a letter to Percy Bush, also provides a fascinating account of the atmosphere in which the game was played, commenting on how the singing had a tremendous effect on the game and highlighting the 'prayers of the more frenzied spectators'. As an Englishman, C N Fretwell admitted that the singing had had an effect on him and that, as a result of the atmosphere and prayer-like singing, Wales could not have possibly lost the match.

The *Daily Mail's* correspondent suggests that the All Blacks failed to make any early impact on the Welsh side because, for the first time, they had met a similar team whose strategy, like theirs, was to attack. Also, unlike other teams they met on the tour, Wales were not in awe of the All Blacks. The two teams were equal in experience, speed and weight. The *Mail* believed the New Zealanders were lulled into a false sense of security. The same art and finesse which they had employed against other teams was now used by their opponents.

The *Daily Mail,* and the press generally, was critical of the play of Mynott at first five-eighth (fly half) who had replaced Stead. They thought he was mesmerised by the crowd and was flurried and harassed by the 'shadow of Cliff Pritchard', the spoiler, whose mission it was to dislocate the 'Five-eighths part of the machine and thus put it out of gear'.

The report highlights that many New Zealand players were visibly upset by the baiting of Gallaher by the crowd, who was also subject to a 'pitless fusillade of epithets' for his style of play. Also, Hunter and Deans, who were usually so safe, failed to take or give passes time after time.

Much has been written about Teddy Morgan's try. Reminiscing in 1946, Rhys Gabe described how the try was created:

> The plan was not to employ Cliff Pritchard, the extra back, in any attacking movement, so as to lull our opponents into a false sense of security. Therefore, whenever Dicky obtained possession he was to serve Percy Bush every time until the time was deemed ripe for the execution to the rule. When the signal was at last given, we four engaged in the experiment, were naturally all agog with excitement and anxiety, for it would be a disaster if anyone blundered after exposing our strategy. Dicky obtained possession and Bush, Nicholls and Llewellyn started running to the right, presumably with the intention of attacking in that quarter. But this was not to be, for Owen, with his inimitable reverse pass, served Pritchard for the first time on the left. Away Cliff, myself and Teddy Morgan sped for dear life. Luckily, no errors were committed in giving and taking the ball and ultimately Teddy darted over the line with the only try of the match.

Following Morgan's try, the *Daily Mail* indicated that 'It seemed that every throat in the Principality from Orme's Head to Milford Haven was celebrating the event'.

Wales continued to have the best of it in the scrum and the backs were creating opportunities, particularly Percy Bush, but Teddy Morgan failed to hold on to potential scoring passes. Meanwhile, Winfield was kicking superbly into touch making 50 to 60 yards, saving his own forwards and running the All Black pack off its legs.

Interestingly, the *Western Mail* reporter makes no reference to the 'Deans incident', while the *Daily Mail* suggests that he was tackled across the Welsh try line: 'though the referee, whose decision is bound to be accepted in such matters, declared that he had been "held up" and ordered a scrum instead of a place kick.' Huw Richards also highlights that Gallaher and Stead failed to mention the incident in their account of the match.

There has been a lot of speculation regarding 'the try' and whether it was scored by Deans or whether he was pulled back by the Welsh players. Again, I do not want to go over old ground but rather present new and independent evidence provided to Percy Bush in previously unpublished letters from a Yorkshire schoolmaster who attended the game with his chums during the Christmas break from St Paul's College, Cheltenham. The letters were written to Bush in March and September 1944, on West Riding County Council headed notepaper, by schoolmaster C N Fretwell, who provided an eyewitness account of the game. He was teaching at St Paul's College (with English rugby international Dai Gent) and decided to travel down to the game prior to returning home to Yorkshire for the

Christmas holidays. He described how he and his friends were first stood at the corner in which 'Deans claimed' he secured a try.

Fretwell addresses all versions of events and is firm in his view that Deans did not score. He offers the following account. Teddy Morgan was the only Welsh player who claimed Deans had scored. Fretwell disputes Teddy Morgan's version as, in his view, 'Dr Morgan was underneath Deans when he grassed him so suddenly or miraculously, for it did seem a certainty that Deans would be going over and I do not think the Doctor would be in such a good position to see (do spectators see more of the game?)'.

E D H Sewell was a leading rugby writer of the time, and often a critic of Welsh tactics. Sewell was sitting in the press box on the halfway line. The same eyewitnesses (including Fretwell) entered into correspondence with Sewell who rejected their views. In his book, *Rugger: The Man's Game*, Sewell described the location of the press table as 'five yards inside touch and the floor of it a good two feet below the level of the pitch'. Fretwell's view (and supported by Sewell's own evidence from his book) was that:

> ... he was hardly in a good position to judge whether a try had been scored at that corner and ridicules my talk of misery and despair on Deans' face and [Sewell] even says he was not laid out full length with outstretched arms reaching for the line with the ball, and that Welsh players dragged him back from over the line after he had crossed!

Sewell also suggested that the silence of the crowd indicated it was a try. Fretwell recalled that there was a tremendous yell as Deans was grassed short of the line – a tremendous yell of joy and relief, 'which quickly died down as the danger to Wales was still evident'.

Fretwell refers to how his brother, who was at the game in the same corner, highlighted 'the look on Deans' face as he lay grassed and stretched out, showed what he himself thought of the moment'. He was short of the line! This account fits the one given by Rhys Gabe which counters Deans' and Teddy Morgan's view, in that Gabe was the tackler and he felt Deans tried to struggle forward, rather than, as he would have done if he had crossed the line, ground the ball. When Deans claimed after the match that he had scored and Gabe asked why he had struggled, 'there was no answer'.

The *Daily Mail* was in no doubt that it was the forwards Wales had to thank for victory. For once, the New Zealanders met a pack as heavy and as skilful as themselves. The *Western Mail* praised the Welsh selection committee whose policy of a new formation of seven forwards and eight backs was completely and absolutely fulfilled.

The newspaper also saw the wisdom of the selection team in falling back upon the great players (Nicholls, Hodges, Llewellyn) who had been subject to 'cheap sneers and jibes of the English press as crocks and veterans, has been fully vindicated'. The *Western Mail*, among others, applauded the great game played by Charlie Pritchard, commenting that, 'His deadly tackling was chiefly the means of preventing the attack of the colonial backs being fully developed on a single occasion'. Following the game, the *Daily Mail* highlighted the celebrations: 'Every restaurant and fruit shop and pastry establishment was raided after the match and until late in the evening, the streets were filled with demonstrative crowds all rejoicing in Wales' historic victory and downfall of the invincibles.' They had no doubt the best team had won: 'through their superior excellence and through steadfast Cymric hearts.'

Controversy still persists today, while 'The Game' is regarded by many as the greatest international rugby match ever played, this is also conveyed in the worldwide interest in any item of memorabilia that goes on sale relating to the match. However, it will long be remembered as a landmark game for both countries. Huw Richards states:

> Whereas most nation's [sic] great moments are somebody else's misery, Wales v New Zealand in 1905 is shared, a defining moment for New Zealand, a new nation, and for Wales, an old one that had undergone a profound transformation over the previous half century and for who rugby, in the absence of more conventional institutions, was becoming the main means of collective national self-expression.

In playing only eight times for Wales, Percy falls a long way behind in terms of appearances by other Number 10s who have played for Wales. However, there is no doubt that in his short international career he provided great entertainment, displayed supreme skill and left his mark in the most celebrated rugby international of all time.

CHAPTER 6

Blue and Black – Glory and Despair

THERE IS NO doubt that Percy Bush was one of the most successful captains Cardiff RFC ever had. He played 171 games for the 'Blue and Blacks' between 1899/1900 and 1913/14, scored 66 tries, 25 drop goals and one penalty goal and captained them in three seasons 1905–6, 1906–7 and 1908–9. This period as captain was associated with one of the most successful eras in the club's history, when the side met and defeated the South African and Australian teams in 1907 and 1908 respectively, and lost only narrowly to the great All Blacks team of 1905.

Percy was to play a crucial role in both the victories and the narrow defeat. His three periods as captain were immensely successful as the following analysis shows:

	Played	Won	Lost	Drew	For	Against
1905–06	32	29	1	2	513	86
1906–07	30	25	3	2	404	83
1908–09	31	26	3	2	372	138
Total	93	80	7	6	1,289	307

In terms of performance measures, Percy's record

stands out for the number of victories (86 per cent), beating the record of captain Gwyn Nicholls (74 per cent over four seasons between 1898 and 1903) and Jack Matthews (76 per cent record over three seasons between 1945 and 1951), all successful captains who led the club three or more times and during great periods in the club's history.

The choice of Percy as captain was not just based on his skill as a rugby player and his match winning, he was also immensely popular off the field and loved by players and spectators alike. Danny Davies, the club historian, reflecting on the great 1905 season, referred to Percy's unbridled confidence and how he inspired his men. J B G Thomas acknowledged that Bush was one of the most amazing personalities ever to lead the club. Writing in 1976, he indicated that 'today he would have been a personality of many parts and certainly a TV star'.

There is little doubt that in reading and researching contemporary correspondence from fans and players that he was revered: 'His diminutive stature, puckish humour, love of the practical joke and match-winning abilities all combined to produce a character who endeared himself to his players and fans alike, but not to administrators,' claimed J B G Thomas.

His club career captured all of the above characteristics but perhaps it is his performance against the three major touring teams of 1905, 1907, and 1908 which encapsulate his talent, humour, and frailties in great measure and, particularly, his apparent 'mistake' against the 1905 All Blacks versus the Cardiff club, which also generated some poignant responses from his fans, criticisms from his detractors, and a recently discovered confession from Percy himself. The teams that day were as follows:

	Cardiff RFC	New Zealand
Full back	H B Winfield	W J Wallace
Three-quarters	J L Williams	H D Thomson
	E G Nicholls	R G Deans
	R T Gabe	E E Booth
	R Thomas	J Hunter
	R A Gibbs	J W Stead
Halfbacks	P Bush (capt.)	
	D David	F Roberts
Forwards	W Neill	F Glasgow
	G Northmore	S Casey
	J Powell	F Newton
	F Smith	A McDonald
	J Brown	G W Nicholson
	L George	J J O'Sullivan
	E Rumbelow	C Seeling
		D Gallaher (capt.)

For Cardiff, Gareth Nicholls and Ralph Thomas scored tries, with Winfield converting one. For New Zealand, Thompson and Nicholson scored tries. Wallace converted both.

The game against the All Blacks on Boxing Day (after the game against Wales the previous Saturday), attracted a larger crowd, and while Cardiff lost 10–8 and became the only side to score two tries against the All Blacks on tour, the game will be remembered for a reported error made by Bush in failing to ground the ball over the line after a kick ahead, which allowed Nicholson, the New Zealander forward, to fall on the ball and score. Despite playing brilliantly thereafter, Bush's mistake had cost the game.

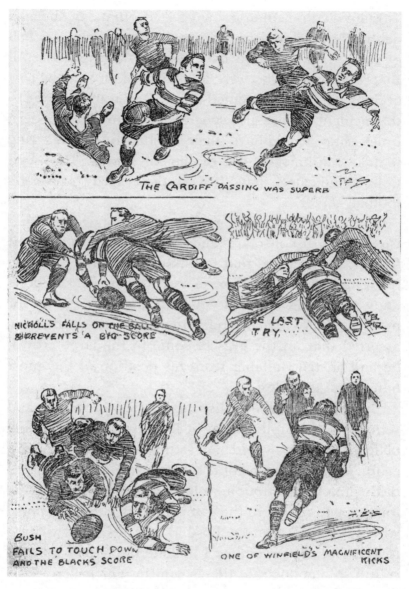

How the local newspapers recorded Percy's 'error' in the New Zealand game.

Many commentators suggested that Bush had deliberately delayed his efforts to touch down the ball or clear it, in order to have the last laugh on the All Blacks forwards who were following up. 'It was the sort of thing he did,' commented Danny Davies in referring to the incident. Davies also suggested that in these modern times critics would have suggested that Bush was trying to take the 'mickey' out of the All Blacks. Townsend Collins indicated that, 'It was the tragedy of Bush's football career'.

Following the game, press reports suggested that Bush was disconsolate and the *Western Mail* went further and claimed that in talking about the incident, tears had welled up in Percy's eyes as he said, 'I don't know why I did it, but it will be a lifelong memory for me'. The *Daily Mail*, in referring to the Bush mistake, asserted that, in the eyes of some in the large crowd, he had ousted Gallaher from his position of the 'most hated man in Wales'.

Bush was apparently distraught after the match, and retired to his family home in Romilly Crescent. Many believed that he would not return to play for Cardiff again. While the focus of comment was initially critical of Bush, a wave of public sentiment followed, pleading for Percy to return to the game and the club, an appeal which included even the Lord Mayor of Cardiff writing to Percy on 29 December. I include the letter's content in full to demonstrate the esteem in which Percy was held:

Dear Mr Bush,

I feel I cannot allow this opportunity to pass without heartedly congratulating you and the members of the Cardiff Football Team on their magnificent display against the New Zealanders on Tuesday last. This match proved conclusively that Welsh Club Football is not one whit inferior to the International Organisation of our sister Colony.

At the same time I desire to extend to you my sincere sympathy in the misfortune which befell you. It is one of these most unfortunate mistakes which inevitably occur in the field of sport and your one little sin of omission must be weighed in the scale of the many fine exhibitions of the rugby code which it has been my pleasure to witness. I can appreciate the keen regret you must feel at the occurrence but still there is the consolation that the Cardiff team lost none of its prestige on Tuesday's encounter and did what all other teams in the four countries failed to do; viz crossed the New Zealand's line twice. This fact alone reflects unbounded credit on the Cardiff team considering the very tall scores the New Zealanders have placed against English country and club teams. I sincerely hope you will take fresh heart and again lead your team which has done so well this season to victory in the remaining matches.

With best wishes for the New Year and for your speedy recovery to your usual health.

Believe me, to be yours, very faithfully.

Robert Hughes
Lord Mayor of Cardiff

29 December 1905

Please let me add this – you are in my opinion the cleverest halfback playing today.

Prior to the intervention of the Lord Mayor, Percy received a letter from W R Jones, Llanelly, possibly Pussy Jones who played for Wales in the late 1890s. It read as follows:

Cheer up old man! We do not know of any other great player who has had a similar experience. They come to all – just ask Bancroft, A J Gould, Gwyn Nicholls etc. It happens to be your turn now. In the near future it will be someone else's turn. The twentieth century has seen and will see many strange things, but it has not and will not see a perfect football player. I heartedly wish many so-called 'football critics' would realise this.

Yours sincerely

W R Jones

A Mr D C Lewis of Newcastle Emlyn, an ordinary supporter who was at the game, offered solace to Percy:

I am sorry to understand that you have allowed the slight error you committed on Tuesday to affect you to such an extent. Mistakes will happen. You played cleverly throughout and some of your runs were simply electrifying.

Yours faithfully

D C Lewis

The letters from all parts of Wales not only demonstrate the warmth of affection felt for Bush but also how the age of sporting superstars had already begun, and the level of fan worship associated with the game in the early part of the twentieth century.

Percy eventually returned to play for Cardiff against Moseley on 10 February and the press reports confirmed he had 'a magnificent reception'. He went on to score four tries and kicked three goals in a 32–0 victory.

However, while 'the mistake' was well documented by the press and contemporary rugby writers, new evidence has emerged from notes written by Percy Bush in his own copy of C S Arthur's *The Cardiff Rugby Football Club*

History and Statistics 1876–1906 (unearthed in Australia) relating to the account of the game versus New Zealand. In his own handwriting, he describes as 'rubbish' the account of the game which suggested that the 'Cardiff captain lost his head'. Percy boasted: 'the Cardiff captain never did. It was simply a function of the balls dipping awkwardly,' but even so (Percy claimed) no try was actually scored:

> Seeling and Glasgow fell on the ball but the ball, ground and hand were never 'in momentary contact' until in fact ball, ground and hand were brought into contact by the Cardiff captain. Gil Evans' decision was quite wrong, it should have been a restart as the Cardiff captain was the only one who touched down the ball in accordance with the laws of rugby.

> Signed
> F Percy Bush
> Captain Cardiff RFC
> 2 January 1907

> P.S. As will be gathered the incident took place from the far out, when the referee arrived at the spot I was actually in possession of the ball.

This is a remarkable confession and has not been noted in any of the contemporary reports of the game or in any subsequent analysis of the match. Clearly, Percy's strongly-worded response and his signature suggests he feels he was badly treated at the time, while history firmly identifies him as the 'villain'. Following the Deans controversy a few days earlier, perhaps Percy thought that his version of events would be seen as a distraction and an attempt by Wales to balance the errors?

The victory over South Africa in January 1907

is regarded as one of the Cardiff club's greatest performances. The game was the last one for the South Africans on their United Kingdom itinerary and was played in horrendous conditions as a result of many days of torrential rain. Despite covering the pitch with straw, Paddy Carolin, the vice captain of the tour party, described the pitch as though a river had overflowed; the ground was literally a sea of mud at least a foot deep.

The Cardiff team and particularly the key international players, Nicholls and Bush, had been smarting from the defeat of Wales at Swansea earlier in the season and the criticism they had received. So much so, Nicholls came out of retirement to play and to re-establish his reputation. Percy, writing in 1938, indicated that Nicholls came out of retirement and played 'as a personal favour to me as Captain of Cardiff'. Nicholls implied to Paddy Carolin that careful thought had gone into the selection of the Cardiff team following the Wales defeat. However, the team had suffered a blow as Bush had not played since the Welsh defeat, as he'd had his tonsils removed in October, a particularly difficult operation and recuperation for an adult in 1907.

Looking back at the game in the 1940s, Percy thought the Springboks 'were easily the best of any colonial teams ever to visit our shores for pure, clean methods and sportsmanship in the highest meaning of the word, not to forget the quality of their play, which I consider to have surpassed that of any of the others (either before or since)'. He adds:

... in the early morning of New Year's day, I was awakened by sheets of rain trying to crack the windows of my bedroom. Excellentisimo, says I, and gratefully go off to sleep again. For sodden grounds make little difference to Cardiff players, we being used to them, while our poor South African cousins are very little accustomed to such.

Percy described how the violent rain continued all day supported by 'half a gale of wind' just to help. By the time of the kick off everyone, but the few under covers, was soaked to the bone. The teams were as follows:

	Cardiff	South Africa
Full back	H B Winfield	A F W Marsberg
Three-quarters	C Biggs	J Loobser
	R T Gabe	G J Hirsch
	E G Nicholls	H A de Villiers
	J L Williams	A C Stegmann
Halfbacks	P F Bush (capt.)	D C Jackson
	R A Gibbs	F J Dobbin
	D David	
Forwards	A Brice	P Roos (capt.)
	G Northmore	J W Raaff
	J Powell	D J Brink
	F Smith	H J Daneel
	J Brown	D F T Morkel
	J Casey	D S Mare
	W Neill	P LeRoux
		W A Millar

Unsurprisingly, Percy won the toss and asked the South Africans to play against the rain and wind in the first half.

Cardiff had discussed tactics and decided to play three halves, Percy, Dicky Morgan, and Reggie Gibbs, tactics first employed successfully against the All Blacks in 1905. Other commentators felt it was initiated to accommodate Nicholls' return without upsetting the regular backs. This is doubtful, as sentiment would not have got in the way of a potential victory over a major touring team and, importantly, avenging the insult to Wales and restoring the reputations of Bush and Nicholls. Bush stood deep from the scrum away from the tacklers, with Gibbs taking the tackles and bangs. Paddy Carolin was intrigued by the selection of three halves, however its full impact was never seen as Gibbs was injured early following a collision with Miller, and was a passenger for the rest of the game. The conditions also made it difficult to establish where the playing of three halves influenced the outcome of the game. Bush, apparently, amused the spectators as he attempted to avoid being tackled on the treacherous surface.

This was the great Gwyn Nicholls' last game. He never played another big match but many commentators, including the South African team, regarded his final game as the most brilliant of his career. In looking back, Percy described how in the first ten minutes:

> Nicholls got a sweet pass from Rusty Gabe, broke through the centre and bore down on the great (in every sense) A F Marsburg, the full back. For the only time I had known, Gwyn did not give his wing a simple walk over. He would not risk a pass with a ball as heavy as lead already, and as slippery as an eel – then some. He handed off Marsburg as though he had been 7 stone not 14 stone, and scored a try which sent real warmth into the blood of the spectators who went wild.

The game was also notable for the performance of the great South African full back, Marsberg, who was carried from the field at Swansea by Welsh supporters and, following the Cardiff game, a crowd of 9,000 assembled outside the team's hotel and carried him shoulder high to the station.

For Cardiff, Nicholls, Gibbs, Williams and Gabe scored tries, with Winfield kicking a penalty and conversion to win, 17–0. The South Africans, despite the conditions, admitted they had been thoroughly and absolutely outplayed. The result was significant in a number of ways. For the first time on the tour, the South Africans failed to score against a club or country side and secondly, Cardiff's winning margin of 17 points still remains to this day one of South Africa's heaviest defeats on a tour of Britain, Ireland and France. Dave Guiney highlighted the fact that the South Africans were only beaten again by a margin of 17 points in 1965, and that in New Zealand when they were defeated 6–23 by Wellington.

The visit of the first Australian side in 1908, christened the Wallabies, was the first in a series of games which had seen the club maintain a remarkable record of never having lost to a touring Australian side. Again, because of the 'demands' of the professional age, this record is likely to persist as the opportunities for clubs to play touring teams is now significantly reduced. The Australian team of 1908 finished the tour with a record of: played 38, won 32, drawn one and lost five.

Compared to the visits of the 1905 All Blacks and 1906 South African team, the Wallaby record was not as good, but they did play exciting and attacking football and brought great pleasure to spectators throughout England and Wales. The tour was a success financially, grossing £3,000, and the *South Wales Daily Post* also thought the tourists had a larger and more varied experience of rugby in Wales than the All Blacks had in 1905, because they not only played the coastal teams but the hill teams too, who the paper claimed were experts on their own grounds.

The long-running feud between the English Rugby Union and the Scottish and Irish Unions meant that no invitations were forthcoming for the Australian team in either of the latter countries, on the basis that their daily allowance rate meant that they were 'deemed professionals'.

Yet, while the 1905 and 1906 tours have been covered extensively by writers and journalists, the 1908 tour had probably as much 'on field' and 'off field' dramas as the 1905 tour, not just because of the espionage and intrigue associated with illegal approaches to the team from both the Northern Union (Rugby League) and the New South Wales Rugby League. This situation led to the defection of many of the 1908 stars to rugby league, which in turn caused the demise of rugby union in Australia. Rugby league became the premier code of rugby, as it is still to this day.

While the background drama was playing out, the team who played in blue and wore the badge of the waratah were persuaded by management (much to the annoyance of players) to develop a 'war cry' imitating the New Zealand team of 1905. This preceded almost every tour match and was also performed during after-match dinners and smoking concerts, to the enjoyment of the spectators and audience.

The team, however, was embarrassed by the 'antics' and regarded it as the 'gravest affliction'. Herbert Moran, captain of the side, recounted in his autobiography,

Viewless Winds, that in response to performing the war song he 'regularly hid among the team, a conscientious objector...' The team also participated in the 1908 Olympics and won the gold medal for rugby union, defeating Cornwall (representing England) 32–3 in the final.

Of the five games lost on tour, four of these were in Wales, against Cardiff, Llanelly, Swansea, and Wales, while the one draw was against Abertillery. The victory of Cardiff, by 24–8, was their heaviest defeat of the tour.

Cardiff's preparations for the game against the Australians on 28 December were disrupted by illness, injuries and the weather. Percy Bush was recovering from a bout of influenza, while Sgt Fred Smith had to drop out because of a rheumatic attack, and Bert Winfield had dislocated his thumb against the Barbarians the previous Saturday.

The weather turned colder and the Australians were greeted by a real snowstorm on arriving in Cardiff. The Cardiff club used many of the city's unemployed to clear the pitch, and braziers to ensure the game could be played. Hamish Stuart, an English reporter, indicated that Australia were well beaten, particularly up front, while the Cardiff backs were admirable. The teams were as follows:

	Cardiff	Australia
Full back	R F Williams	P P Carmichael
Three-quarters	R A Gibbs	C J Russell
	L M Dyke	J Hickey
	J L Williams	E Mandible
	W J Spiller	F Bede Smith
Halfbacks	P F Bush (capt.)	F Wood

	W L Morgan	C H McKivat
Forwards	J Pugsley	H Moran (capt.)
	J Brown	N Row
	J Powell	A B Burge
	J Casey	S A Middleton
	J Daley	P McCue
	G Yewlett	M McCarthur
	F Gaccon	C Hammand
	D Westacott	J T Barnett

For Cardiff, tries were scored by J L Williams (2), Morgan, Gibbs and Dyke. Bush dropped a goal and kicked a penalty and a conversion. For Australia, Hickey and Moran scored tries, with Carmichael kicking a conversion.

At the start of the game, in response to the Australian war cry, Percy Bush decided to counter the team by brandishing a Zulu sword and shield (as noted, reputedly a relic from Rorke's Drift). Old Stager reported that it was an amusing incident, and he stopped short of doing any damage. He also thought that Bush's captaincy was an example of perfect generalship and set an inspiring example to his men. From time to time during the game, Reggie Gibbs, a right winger, would step into the space normally occupied by Bush, which apparently confused the Australians, a tactic carried over from the win against South Africa.

Dyke's try was scored following a move by Bush who 'had beat everyone apart from the full back'.

The match was also notable for the sending off of the Australian forward, Albert Burge, for kneeing Westacott in the groin. Gil Evans, the referee, ordered Burge from the field to a backdrop of booing from the large crowd.

This was the third sending off during the tour. While initially unsettled, the tourists pulled back to 14–8 but Percy decided to retaliate through more attacking play, and Cardiff eventually ran out winners, 24–8. Towards the end of the game, the crowd from the 'sixpenny' side chanted the refrain, 'Who beat the Wallabies? Car... Car... Cardiff.'

After the final whistle, the *Western Mail* reported that a tremendous sense of excitement was witnessed. Bush was carried aloft and handled as skilfully as the Welsh three-quarters could nurse the ball. Hundreds of spectators were trying to touch Bush and, after they had stroked his curly locks, they appeared to be satisfied.

Following the game, both sides dined together at the Queen's Hotel, and then opted to watch *Cinderella* at the New Theatre before being overwhelmed by another snowstorm which engulfed most of the southern United Kingdom and caused the abandonment of their next game against Monmouthshire.

The win against Australia kicked off a remarkable series of wins for Cardiff RFC over subsequent Australian touring teams which, with the advent of professional rugby, and the demise of long tours, is likely never to be emulated again.

CHAPTER 7

Sojourn in France
and Later Years

WHETHER THROUGH CHOICE or because the decision was
made for him, Percy's international career ended in 1910.
Thus began a new stage in the life of Bush. His marriage
to a local Cardiff girl, Adeline Wood, on 23 January
1909, precipitated a new path and challenges. Still not
forgetting his humorous side, he signed the solemnization
certificate at St John's Church, Canton, as 'the victim'.
Percy's affection for Adeline was clearly demonstrated in
the previous season when, as noted, in front of a packed
Arms Park, he escorted her across the pitch from the old
pavilion to a place in the women's section.

He worked as a teacher in Wood Street School close
to the Arms Park. It was apparent to many, particularly
in the city's business community, that his marketing
potential could be diverted into other areas. He was
'encouraged' by some coal agents with strong interests
in France to apply for a position as a vice consul in
Nantes.

It was not a coincidence that Percy was prompted
to apply for a position in Nantes. In commercial terms,
France was a leading importer of Welsh coal. In 1900, 71

per cent of all coal exports from Wales went to France and the Mediterranean. By 1911, 2.7 million tons were exported to France. Nantes was also the location where the French government tested Welsh steam coal and, as a result of such tests, Wales replaced the north of England as official supplier to the French government.

There was a joint rugby and commercial objective to Percy's move. Veteran French international Pascal Laporte, former captain of Bordeaux, the five-time French club champions between 1888 and 1907, managed to bring together two local teams to form Stade Nantais University Club, building a competitive team in a remote rugby outpost in north-west France. Recent research indicates that Laporte was also a businessman (importer and exporter of coal). Percy's move to Nantes would address both the commercial and rugby objectives of Laporte and also encourage and support a key export market for south Wales.

Percy was a well-known rugby character in France. Extracts from the *Cardiff Pals Battalion Newspaper* during the First World War refer to conversations between the Cardiff Pals and their colleagues in the French army – Percy Bush's talent was acclaimed by both sets of soldiers. Such a household name could certainly help promote Welsh commercial interest. He was appointed a pro consul in Nantes on 19 October 1918. He went on to become vice consul in December 1924, and was acting consul there from 1911 to 1936 before resigning in 1937 and returning to Cardiff due to ill health.

During his French sojourn, he continued his rugby career and made a spectacular impact on rugby in

Nantes and France through his involvement as a player with Stade Nantais University Club. As in Wales, he was feted by local newspapers, as photographs and cartoons illustrate, no doubt influenced not only by his reputaton in Wales and the United Kingdom, but also by the 57 points he scored in 1910 against Saint-Nazaire for the University Club – 7 tries, 4 drop goals, 2 penalties and 7 conversions. Recognising his international profile, *The Times* in London announced to its readers in September 1919 that Percy had been elected captain of Stade Nantais University Club.

Newspapers in north-west France were quick to recognise Percy's talent and his contribution to the game in the region. Prior to the 1911 game versus Stade Bordelais, the local newspaper referred to Percy as the 'best halfback in France at the present time'. His dodging swerves and kicking were without comparison, and his team, it was reported, should go far in that year's championship in France. The pre-match report looked forward to seeing 'the wonderful Percy Bush' leading his backline against the Bordelais team. Prior to another game Percy is referred to as 'a little marvel'.

A further press commentary prior to the game against Bordeaux reminds the newspaper readership that, 'this [Stade Nantais University] club possesses the best pair of halves in France and everybody will want to see the wonderful Percy Bush lead his backline and respond to the assault from the kicking game of the opponents'. The writer reminds readers that Percy had managed, in the last few minutes, to save the game against Toulouse, and was responsible for easily beating local rivals, FC Yonnais, to win the championship of the Atlantic. 'One can be sure that on Sunday he will do his best to stand up to the 15 of Bordeaux.'

After another victory, the local newspaper sang Percy's praises in a report which contains echoes of the commentaries in New Zealand and Australia in 1905:

> Bush was best, that is to say, the extraordinary man we know. He did more than the rest of his three-quarters put together. His relieving kicks to touch saved the team from Nantes, time and time again.

His performances and those of the side helped to promote the cause of rugby in the Atlantic region and in France. He was joined at the club by Mr Mog Richards, a friend and former Cardiff RFC colleague. Richards played for the Cardiff club first XV 78 times between 1907 and 1914.

France made spectacular progress in the Five Nations Championship from being whipping boys in the early part of the twentieth century to their emergence as champions for the first time in 1953/4. Percy, of course, played against the first French rugby visitors to Wales when Stade Français visited Cardiff in April 1905. The French team amused spectators by wearing cut-down coloured trousers and tackling the Cardiff players by holding on to their beards. To Percy's delight, rugby in France progressed, aided by his notable contribution, both on and off the field.

French rugby and the International Rugby Board (IRB) had a difficult relationship from 1913 through to the 1950s. Much of the IRB's concerns focused on veiled professionalism, foul play and the general administration of the game. Scotland cancelled its fixtures with France between 1913 and 1918 due to the 'reprehensible' behaviour of spectators and unsatisfactory stewarding arrangements during and after their game in January 1913, when the spectators invaded the pitch and attacked the referee. Scottish players were struck by stones. France was expelled from the IRB in 1932, but reinstated in 1939. Allegation of foul play and professionalism were upheld. The IRB continued to keep a watchful eye on French rugby yet, in 1952, they were close to being expelled once again, but were saved by the support of Wales. Much of the Welsh support for France was down to not only the WRU recognising the same pressures which were directed towards them, particularly in the early years of the century, but also lobbying from within, notably by Percy Bush who had a close affinity with French rugby officialdom and players.

The IRB were putting pressure on the French to disband their club championship, believing it was encouraging violent play and nurturing professionalism. Percy agreed that the championship should be dissolved but disagreed that professionalism was encouraged by the championship – having himself played in it.

Percy, in 1938 correspondence, describes how England, Scotland and Ireland were determined to drop fixtures against France long before the actual rupture. He goes on to highlight that one of the reasons they were disgruntled was because 'France had grown up in the rugby world and was no longer an easy victim'. He goes on to describe how Wales remained true to the French until the 1930 international at Stade Colombes where 'the intense vigour (to call it by a euphemistic title) of certain French players caused even us to consider that it was time to call a halt in the interests of the game on both sides of the channel'. Percy highlighted that things were done that day which were without precedent in international football. The game was played in front of a crowd of 50,000, the largest ever for a rugby match in France. A win for France would have given them the Five Nations tournament for the first time. The game was heavily punctuated with foul play from both sides, with the Welsh hooker receiving nine stitches after being kicked in the face. The press in England and France condemned the brutality of the game. *The Times* wrote: 'An attractive game at Colombes is a very rare spectacle. Frenchmen who are keen supporters of the rugby game… are showing some alarm lest the international matches played here should be allowed to degenerate to the level of their own regional championships, in which some of them see the true cause of the decline.'

Percy worked tirelessly behind the scenes to support France between the 1930s and 1950s and put pressure on Tommy Vile and the WRU to support the French cause, particularly after 1931 when the British Unions discontinued fixtures. Correspondence between the two players indicate that Vile, with his strong IRB connections, regularly referred to 'this France business' and, writing in 1952, Vile implores Percy to provide him with a view on 'our decision regarding France'. He also indicated that he met Percy's 'French Pals' in Dublin and 'they had to be spoken to very strongly'.

There is no doubt that in these troubled times for French rugby, with concerns about professionalism and violence in the game, Percy worked hard in the background to encourage both the IRB and the French Rugby Union to get together to resolve the situation. Unsurprisingly, Percy was awarded the silver Medal of Honour (Médaille d'argent de le Reconnaissance Française) by the French government for this contribution to Anglo-French relations in 1952.

Similarly, when Vile was standing to become the president of the WRU, a particularly bitter battle on that occasion, he encouraged Percy to 'lobby clubs' in order to nominate Vile as he could not nominate himself. Vile became president of the WRU in 1955/6.

Throughout his playing career, during retirement and up until his death, Percy kept in regular touch with survivors of the 1904 Anglo-Australian tour, known as the 'Old Crocks'. This nickname was ascribed to the tourists following the New Zealand stage of that tour when through key injuries, especially to the captain Bedell-Sivright and others, a team had to be patched up to play.

Percy's great friend, scrum half for Wales and confidant from his early playing days, was Tommy Vile of Newport. Both had been uncapped tourists in 1904. They played for the first time together for Wales in 1908 in the Triple Crown win against Scotland. Vile holds the distinction of playing pre and post the First World War for Wales and was captain against Scotland in 1921 at the grand old age of 37. Other core 'Old Crocks' included Arthur O'Brien, Charlie Patterson, Willie Llewellyn, Bernard Massey, Jack Fisher, and Rhys Gabe.

On many occasions they managed to get together to celebrate their friendship and memories, the last meeting taking place in 1950, three years before Percy passed away. Writing in 1949, Arthur O'Brien recalled that 'we had no quarrels or disputes (during the 5 to 6 months away) although we were brought together haphazardly'. The 'Old Crocks' also used their contacts and fame effectively to achieve some collective and personal objectives relating to rugby football in the 1940s and 1950s. Certainly, the Welsh contingent, such as Percy Bush and Tommy Vile, conspired on a number of issues and both helped each other achieve some notable objectives.

After returning to Cardiff and the family home in Romilly Crescent in 1938 due to ill health, Percy had a range of employment, including being a press reporter on rugby and cricket games for local and national newspapers, such as *The News of the World*. His fame and reputation also saw him employed by the Rediffusion Company which supplied most south Wales family homes with the standard wireless sets of the 1940s and 1950s. Percy had a marketing role and also 'lent' his famous 1905 jersey for inclusion in window displays in Rediffusion shops all over south Wales. He also had a spell as a welfare officer at the famous Cardiff factory of Curran's Engineering which, not surprisingly, had strong associations with the Cardiff club via supporters and former players. Curran's employees would have regarded him as a hero. A good recruitment strategy.

He also petitioned the WRU regularly for a job as an 'official advisor' to report on emerging players across and outside Wales and those 'addicted to "ungentle" methods unlikely to bring Wales into disrepute'. Needless to say, his requests were ignored.

There is evidence that this rugby genius seems to have had some difficulty in settling down and finding employment opportunities that would keep him fully occupied. His health had also deteriorated, not aided by his smoking habit, while his children, Coralie and Louis, regularly claimed in correspondence that the climate in Cardiff did not help him. In reviewing correspondence from the 1940s through to his death, it was clear that he continued to be adored by fans and personalities. A letter from the famous cricket commentator, John Arlott, in response to one from Percy begins: 'A letter from you is a souvenir to be hoarded.' Percy was made president of Cardiff RFC Supporters' Club in the 1950s.

After the death of Percy's wife Adeline in October 1941, Coralie and Louis stayed with Percy, and remained unmarried for the rest of their lives. Both were intelligent and fluent in languages, but Louis particularly found difficulty in settling down to a job on returning from France. Many of Percy's friends were approached. Initially, Louis showed an inclination towards working in the arts in London, but a friend of Percy commented that 'Louis doesn't know anything about hard work or the hard factors of life. I am certain that if he had gone into a London studio ... it would have broken his heart in a week'.

Louis was referred to as 'quite brilliant' but was handicapped by his continental education and training. One of Percy's London contacts suggested that Louis should not spend too much time in Cardiff because it was the 'city of the dead'. Percy, writing in 1935 prior to his departure from France, was keen to fix Coralie with a position and wrote to many of his friends. The Second World War decided Louis' fate and he enlisted in the Intelligence Corps. Throughout the war his language skills and intelligence served him well. From the limited information available, it appears that Louis may have shared some of his aunt's views on the merits of war.

From a rugby perspective, Percy had views on both players and tactics. A strong sense comes through his correspondence, newspaper articles and his one-and-only contribution to a coaching book on rugby, Cliff Jones' 1937 book *Rugby Football*, of his frustration with the then modern game and the skill of players.

In his general correspondence, particularly with Vile, he was critical of a number of leading Welsh players of the day. He described John Gwilliam, Wales captain and second row forward, as 'an absolute fool and not a captain. He used to make me laugh.' Similarly, in evaluating Cliff Morgan, the Wales, British Lions and Cardiff fly half, Percy described him as a player who 'runs anywhere and never knows where he is'. In 1949 he applauds Haydn Tanner, the Cardiff and Wales scrum half, as one of the best since his former partner Dicky David in terms of speed of pass. He describes Bleddyn Williams, the Cardiff, Wales and Lions centre, as 'superlative'.

Most of his thoughts on 'modern rugby' and comparisons with the old game were included in Cliff Jones' coaching book and among the articles he wrote for local newspapers. He covered many themes and often wrote under the nom de plume, Secundus. They make interesting reading, particularly today, and help provide a further insight into Percy's approach to the game and his technical awareness. They also offer an intriguing insight into the game during the first Golden Era. As you would expect, the game in this era is generally viewed positively; however, some of his views on the technical deficiencies of the 'modern player' and game are relevant today.

In terms of fitness, he criticised the modern player for playing to get fit. He emphasised how he and his Cardiff colleagues would train two evenings per week, as well as doing weight training and skipping. He deplores 'the preference for cocktail parties among players of today'. (What would he think of today's players' social lifestyles?)

From a playing perspective, even in 1937 he was critical of the mechanistic nature of play and appears exasperated that 'moves' were planned well before the day of the match. While he acknowledged that unorthodox play may not have sat comfortably with selectors, he questioned the need and trend for scrum halves to dive pass, claiming that by doing so they took themselves out of the game. He disagreed with the trend towards specialists, particularly in the forwards. In the Golden Era, forwards were interchangeable and some could, and did, play in all positions in the scrum. Percy also highlighted (as in today's game) the curse of cross-field running, which he claimed was a modern phenomena. He also criticised the inability of players to kick with both feet and the trend towards high tackles.

From a rules perspective, he deplored the failure of referees to penalise 'foot up' in the scrums, while again highlighting how referees failed to allow advantage from the knock-on.

In assessing his comments on players and the modern game, it would appear to many a classic case of an old player looking at his playing days through rose-tinted spectacles, like many a retired international these days.

However, from Bush's perspective, he was comparing two very different games. As many other commentators have recognised, the game played in the Golden Era, particularly in the early years, was a classical game where forwards were there to win the ball for the three-quarters to secure tries. However, the two lines of three-quarters competed against each other without fear of wing forwards closing their space down and interfering with the movement of the ball. A classical game.

In reviewing the modern game, Percy was watching and summarising a game which must have been strange to him. Wing forwards now acted as curbs on three-quarter play, cutting down space and pressing halfbacks and wingers, while forwards had specialist positions and engaged in interplay with the three-quarters.

The decline in three-quarters' skills and cross-field running, identified by Percy, are concerns in today's game. In the classic game played in the Golden Era, Percy did not have to deal with wing forwards pressurising three-quarters, giving them less time and space to use their skills. However, it is clear that the players of the Golden Era did study the game intensely, and referred to a 'scientific thinking'. You only have to read some of the classic coaching books from that time, such as Gallaher and Stead's *The Complete Rugby Footballer on the New Zealand System*, to recognise that players in the early part of the twentieth century were continually thinking of ways to improve their game and skills. This was evidenced by the planning to create the famous try in the 1905 Wales v New Zealand match.

W Rowe Harding, who later became a judge, writing in the 1920s, believed that the poor performance of

Welsh teams in the 1920s was down to not only erratic selection, but a failure to understand the changing strategy of the game, particularly the move towards specialist rules for forwards and the need for a quick heel from the maul areas, which England, in particular, were exploiting. Rowe Harding also criticised those commentators (like Percy) who were advocating a return to principles employed in the first Golden Era which Rowe Harding believed could no longer be endorsed in light of changing tactics.

However, in his writings, Percy also came up with some innovations that were adopted in 2008 and referred to as Experimental Law Variations (ELVs). Writing in a local newspaper in 1938, he recognised that precious minutes were wasted in most matches by the 'thrower in' waiting for the forwards on either side to form a lineout. He advocated removing the law which required the ball to be thrown 'at right angles to the touchline', and instead recommended that the 'thrower in' send the ball to any member of his side, provided that the ball be not thrown forwards. He felt that this would not only save time but remove barging, even then a source of ill-feeling. The ELVs of 2008 finally allowed this.

Percy was also an advocate of some of the rules enjoyed by rugby league – highly unusual for a union man writing in 1938. He advocated the adoption of 13-a-side football to bring 'pep' back into the game, and also the rule which disallowed kicking into touch only directly from inside the 25-yard line, and outside only if the ball did not go directly into touch. Rugby union had to wait until 1968 before this rule change was introduced.

In 1938 Percy had just returned from France to Wales where there was a great deal of economic uncertainty. Rugby league continued to attract players and the economic health of the union game appeared vulnerable with the decline of gates and the threat of club disbandment. On the playing field, according to Percy, 'club football became restrictive, plagued by aimless kicking at halfback, partly in reaction to the increasing role of specialist wing forwards, partly in poor imitation of the matchless, and match winning, short punting of Bennie Osler (South Africa)'.

Percy, as a rugby writer and commentator, had first-hand experience of the problems as he toured south Wales covering matches for local newspapers. Percy was, in many ways, responding to the state of Welsh rugby and looking at ways in which the game could be rejuvenated, while also jolting rugby supporters' memory of the way the game was played in the first Golden Era.

Percy Bush died in 1955, and his coffin was carried shoulder high from the house in Romilly Crescent, Canton, by players from Cardiff RFC and by 'Those he knew personally or had seen him in action, and about whom he had often spoken appreciatively after a match (either seen or heard 'on the radio' or read about in the papers).'

That was not the end of Percy's link to the Cardiff club. His recent election to Cardiff RFC's Hall of Fame, as outlined in the Preface, and the affection shown to him and his memory has become clear while writing this book. It is evidence of his enduring appeal among rugby supporters as Welsh rugby's little marvel.

Epilogue

PERCY BUSH WAS not just a product of Wales' first Golden Era but of the times, the city, and the region which nurtured him and, of course, his remarkable Victorian family.

In researching this book it has become quite clear how Percy and the early rugby stars were feted and adored and were just as popular as the rugby superstars of today. However, that was not reflected in the form of the salary or lifestyle of today's stars, but on reading the letters from fans, both in Wales and overseas, and newspaper articles and photographs/postcards of the time. They were obviously held in a very high esteem. Bush was a truly global rugby superstar. He was well known and had played in France, the United Kingdom, Australia and New Zealand and, like the superstars of today, his fame was used by others commercially as he gained a position in France which helped to promote Welsh coal exports.

The players of this era also thought about the game deeply, and the coaching books written by Gallaher and Stead, Gwyn Nicholls, and Dai Gent at the time illustrate the thinking and insight they brought to 'scientific rugby'. Percy, through his letters and article in Cliff Jones' *Rugby Football*, also contributed to rugby progress and some of his proposals for law changes have been introduced today.

Percy and the players of the first Golden Era also had

the joy of playing 'the perfect game'. At the beginning of the era, the forwards won the ball and left the rest to the three-quarters. What a game that must have been, unencumbered by spoiling back row forwards. Towards the end of the era, changes began to take place but, up until the Great War, the rugby game was still close to the perfect game. Percy was playing for a club and in a country where scientific thinking (including new ways of planning for games) was an integral part of the system. It is no coincidence that Cardiff, as a city, was also at the peak of its economic prowess when new thinking in science, arts and education was emerging.

The city wanted to progress, and it required a game to match its growth. Rugby was the game chosen by the population and supported by the city fathers to demonstrate the ambition of the city and its region. Percy Bush was the personality who typified both the ambition and development of the city. He and his family were forged by the society they grew up in and his confidence, zest and leadership were right for the city at the time.

Rugby politics played a strong part in reducing his appearances for Wales and, much like today, it appears that Bush, the 'wayward genius', failed to convince all of the selectors that, despite his crowd-pleasing performances, his ability to make mistakes was too high a price to pay, even in the first Golden Era.

So what can we learn from Percy Bush, the rugby game and Cardiff and south Wales society at the time, and how does it compare to today?

Well, first of all, the same selection difficulties are apparent for wayward geniuses like Bush in today's game. The reluctance of coaches nowadays to 'fully embrace' such players remains. James Hook in Wales, Danny Cipriani in England, Quade Cooper in Australia, are but a few contemporary examples.

What of the game? As in Percy's day, the game is changing, although more rapidly. The tactics of today, the relish for big hits and the destructive role of forwards, would not find favour from Percy and his contemporaries.

What of Cardiff and Wales rugby? Percy would have been delighted with the recent success of the Wales team in winning four championships in five years between 2005 and 2013, including three Grand Slams. He would also, probably, be bemused on hearing that the All Blacks continue to be the nemesis of Wales. And what of his local club? Like many of us, disappointed at the early statistics of the club in the professional era, we are now pleased they are playing on the 'holy ground' again. What of the WRU? It wouldn't surprise him to hear that the Union and clubs have been in dispute, with the Union trying to enforce their central control on the game, as they have done so since their formation.

How would Percy have adjusted to the cult of media personality today? As J B G Thomas indicated in one of his publications, he was convinced that Percy would have had the qualities to be a TV star today. How television and the media now need a new rugby personality, on and off the pitch, to sell the game and product. His puckish charm and good looks would help him thrive in today's game. And what about some of the stunts, such as challenging the Australian team's war dance 'with a sword and shield'; escorting his fiancée across the pitch to a front row seat. A marketing guru's dream!

Another feature that comes through of the rugby game in Percy's era is the enjoyment and camaraderie he and his contemporaries shared, and how this continued throughout their lives.

Watching my son and grandson play rugby today, I earnestly hope they will continue to enjoy and derive as much pleasure from the rugby game as Percy and his colleagues did.

Bibliography

Preface
W J T Collins, *Rugby Recollections*
J C Jenkins, *Rugby Compendium*
F Keating, *Great Number Tens*
Otago Witness, 1904
Financial Times, 23 May 2004

Chapter 1
M Daunton, *Cardiff Coal Metropolis 1870–1914*
J Davies, *History of Modern Wales*
D H Lewis, *America Made Me Welcome*
Janet Scully, *A Legacy Fulfilled – Howells School, Llandaff 1810–2010*
Sheena Stoddard, *Impressions Bristol Etchers 1910–1935*
Cardiff and Merthyr Guardian, 19 December 1868
Weekly Mail, 1 August 1885
Cardiff Times, 1 April 1905
MAP, 1 December 1906
Evening Express, April 1923
Hywelian Magazine, January 1948
Western Mail, January 1948
Western Mail, 22 February 1982
Percy Bush correspondence (unpublished), Dai Richards

Chapter 2
D Davies, *Cardiff RFC: The Greatest*
G Prescott, *This Rugby Spellbound People – Rugby Football in Nineteenth Century Cardiff and South Wales*
D Smith and G Williams, *Fields of Praise: The Official History of the Welsh Rugby Union, 1881–1981*
Percy Bush letters (unpublished), Ken Poole
Cricketarchive.com

Chapter 3

E H D Sewell, *Rugby Football Update*

Australia
Sydney Mail, 19 June 1904
The Sunday Sun, 26 June 1904
The Sydney Sportsman, June 1904
The Evening News, 4 July 1904
Evening Observer, Brisbane, 8 July 1904
Brisbane Daily Mail, 9 July 1904
Saturday Observer, 9 July 1904
Sydney Morning Herald, 13 July 1904
The Referee, 13 July 1904
Brisbane Courier, 14 July 1904
Daily Mail, Brisbane, 14 July 1904
Saturday Sports Observer, 16 July 1904
The Twoomba Chronicle, 21 July 1904
The Brisbane Courier, 21 July 1904
Saturday Observer, 23 July 1904
Sydney Sportsman, 3 August 1904

New Zealand
The Evening Post, 4 August 1904
The Star, 6 August 1904
Otago Daily Times, 11 August 1904
Otago Witness, 12 August 1904
The Evening Post, 12 August 1904
The New Zealand Times, 13 August 1904
The Evening Post, 15 August 1904
Tarinaki Daily News, 16 August 1904
The Auckland Star, 18 August 1904
'R T Gabe's Reminiscences', *South Wales Echo* (1946)

Chapter 4

Townsend Collins, *Rugby Recollection*
D Davies, *Cardiff RFC: The Greatest*
D Smith and G Williams, *Fields of Praise: History of Welsh Rugby Union*
J B G Thomas, *Illustrated History of Welsh Rugby*
Australia, 1904
New Zealand Times 1904
South Wales Graphic, December 1904
Western Mail, 15 December 1905

The Standard, 5 February 1910
'R T Gabes Reminiscences', *South Wales Echo*, 1946
Percy Bush correspondence (unpublished), Dai Richards

Chapter 5

Huw Richards, *A Game for Hooligans*
Trevor Wignall, *The Strand Magazine*, 1944
Daily Mail, 15 December 1905
Western Mail, 18 December 1905
Percy Bush letters (unpublished), Ken Poole

Chapter 6

C S Arthur, *Cardiff Rugby Club History: 1876–1907* (Percy Bush's copy)
Dave Guiney, *The Dunlop Book of Rugby Union*
Lappe Laubscher and Gideon Nieman (eds), *Carolin papers – A Diary of the 1906–07 Springboks Tour*
H Moran, *Viewless Winds*
Peter Sharpham, *The First Wallabies and the Defection to Rugby League*
J B G Thomas, *Illustrative History of Welsh Rugby*
Western Mail, 18 December 1905
South Wales Graphic, December 1905
South Wales Daily News, December 1908
Percy Bush correspondence (unpublished), Dai Richards

Chapter 7

M J Daunton, *Cardiff Coal Metropolis 1870–1914*
Cliff Jones, *Rugby Football*
Mike Rylance, *The Forbidden Game*
Frederick Humberts article in 'Percy Bush, from Cardiff to Nantes', rugby-pioneers.blog.com
Royan, 11/12 September 1910
Les Sports De L'Ouest, 28 October 1911
Le Populaire, 1912
The Times, 2 January 1913
Cardiff Pals Battalion Newspaper, 1914
Percy Bush letters (unpublished), Ken Poole

Epilogue

D Gallaher and W J Stead, *The Complete Rugby Footballer*
D R Gent, *Rugby Football*
Gwyn Nicholls, *The Modern Rugby Game and How to Play It*